CRE▲TIVE
HOMEOWNER®

basements

step by step

CREATIVE HOMEOWNER®, Upper Saddle River, New Jersey

SMART GUIDE: BASEMENTS

MANAGING EDITOR Fran Donegan
SENIOR GRAPHIC DESIGNER Glee Barre
PROOFREADER Sara Markowitz
PHOTO COORDINATOR Mary Dolan
INDEXER Schroeder Indexing Services
DIGITAL IMAGING SPECIALIST Frank Dyer
SMART GUIDE® SERIES COVER DESIGN Clarke Barre
FRONT COVER PHOTOGRAPHY John Parsekian/CH

CREATIVE HOMEOWNER

VICE PRESIDENT AND PUBLISHER Timothy O. Bakke
ART DIRECTOR David Geer
MANAGING EDITOR Fran J. Donegan
PRODUCTION COORDINATOR Sara M. Markowitz

Current Printing (last digit)
10 9 8 7 6 5 4 3 2 1

Manufactured in the United States of America

Smart Guide: Basements, Second Edition
Library of Congress Control Number: 2009921973
ISBN-10: 1-58011-466-0
ISBN-13: 978-1-58011-466-0

CREATIVE HOMEOWNER®
A Division of Federal Marketing Corp.
24 Park Way
Upper Saddle River, NJ 07458
www.creativehomeowner.com

contents

safety first

Though all the designs and methods in this book have been reviewed for safety, it is not possible to overstate the importance of using safe construction methods. What follows are reminders; some do's and don'ts of basic construction. They are not substitutes for your own common sense.

- *Always* use caution, care, and good judgment when following the procedures described in this book.

- *Always* be sure that the electrical setup is safe; be sure that no circuit is overloaded and that all power tools and electrical outlets are properly grounded. Do not use power tools in wet locations.

- *Always* read container labels on paints, solvents, and other products; provide ventilation, and observe all other warnings.

- *Always* read the manufacturer's instructions for using a tool, especially the warnings.

- *Always* use hold-downs and push sticks whenever possible when working on a table saw. Avoid working short pieces if you can.

- *Always* remove the key from any drill chuck (portable or press) before starting the drill.

- *Always* pay deliberate attention to how a tool works so that you can avoid being injured.

- *Always* know the limitations of your tools. Do not try to force them to do what they were not designed to do.

- *Always* make sure that any adjustment is locked before proceeding. For example, always check the rip fence on a table saw or the bevel adjustment on a portable saw before starting to work.

- *Always* clamp small pieces firmly to a bench or other work surface when using a power tool on them.

- *Always* wear the appropriate rubber or work gloves when handling chemicals, moving or stacking lumber, or doing heavy construction.

- *Always* wear a disposable face mask when you create dust by sawing or sanding. Use a special filtering respirator when working with toxic substances and solvents.

- *Always* wear eye protection, especially when using power tools or striking metal on metal or concrete; a chip can fly off, for example, when chiseling concrete.

- *Always* be aware that there is seldom enough time for your body's reflexes to save you from injury from a power tool in a dangerous situation; everything happens too fast. Be *alert!*

- *Always* keep your hands away from the business ends of blades, cutters, and bits.

- *Always* hold a circular saw firmly, usually with both hands so that you know where they are.

- *Always* use a drill with an auxiliary handle to control the torque when large-size bits are used.

- *Always* check your local building codes when planning new construction. The codes are intended to protect public safety and should be observed to the letter.

- *Never* work with power tools when you are tired or under the influence of alcohol or drugs.

- *Never* cut tiny pieces of wood or pipe using a power saw. Cut small pieces off larger pieces.

- *Never* change a saw blade or a drill or router bit unless the power cord is unplugged. Do not depend on the switch being off; you might accidentally hit it.

- *Never* work in insufficient lighting.

- *Never* work while wearing loose clothing, hanging hair, open cuffs, or jewelry.

- *Never* work with dull tools. Have them sharpened, or learn how to sharpen them yourself.

- *Never* use a power tool on a work-piece—large or small—that is not firmly supported.

- *Never* saw a workpiece that spans a large distance between horses without close support on each side of the cut; the piece can bend, closing on and jamming the blade, causing saw kickback.

- *Never* support a workpiece from underneath with your leg or other part of your body when sawing.

- *Never* carry sharp or pointed tools, such as utility knives, awls, or chisels, in your pocket. If you want to carry such tools, use a special-purpose tool belt with leather pockets and holders.

introduction

Like the old lady who lived in the shoe, sooner or later many homeowners find themselves overcrowded in their homes. Increasing the size of a house, however, doesn't necessarily mean adding on more square footage by building an addition. An unfinished basement provides an ideal opportunity to increase your living space at a fraction of the cost of new construction or purchasing a larger home. And you can use the space to meet the needs of you and your family. A converted basement is the ideal spot for a well-equipped home office or a play-room for the kids. For the growing family, a finished base-ment provides the space necessary for an extra bedroom or a full-size apartment. Many people convert their base-ments into exercise rooms or home theaters.

chapter 1

basement planning

Planning Rooms

According to building codes, all habitable rooms must have at least 70 square feet of area with no less than 84 inches in each horizontal direction. This standard is met easily, so from a practical standpoint, the size of most rooms is governed primarily by the size of the furnishings to be used. After all, a 70-square-foot bedroom is hardly a suitable location for a double bed. Keep in mind that the lack of abundant natural light in a basement can make rooms seem more cramped than they might seem elsewhere, so do not assume that the comfortable small room upstairs will feel the same if replicated downstairs.

Building codes also require that a basement room have a minimum ceiling height of 90 inches over at least one half of the room. The only exceptions are bathrooms, kitchens, and hallways, which can have a ceiling height of 84 inches. If a quick measurement between the basement floor and the underside of the joists does not show at least that much headroom, it probably is not possible to obtain a permit to do the work.

Be sure to run phone wiring into the basement so that it is not necessary to sprint up a flight of stairs every time the phone rings. Wiring is installed easily, so plan to include modular jacks in several locations, particularly if the basement space is large.

Planning a Bathroom

A bathroom can be small and yet serviceable at the same time. According to building codes, the headroom in a bathroom can be as low as 84 inches. (That is 6 inches lower than the standard for other rooms.) In most cases, the location of the bathroom is determined by the accessibility of plumbing (drain, waste, and vent lines) and ventilation (an outside window or mechanical ventilation). The plumbing is easier to install and less expensive if it can be tied into existing drain and vent pipes. Usually it is the addition of a toilet that most complicates a basement bathroom because it requires a bigger drain line than a sink or shower. Many people find that a basement shower, in addition to a sink and a toilet, is a considerable convenience, particularly if the basement contains a bedroom or two.

While there may not be much of a view, basements usually contain enough space to hold a large master suite or a good-size guest bedroom.

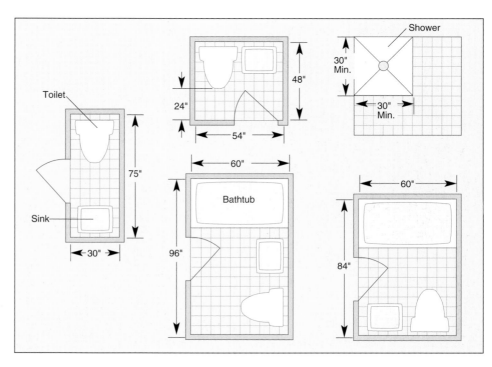

Planning a Bathroom. These are minimum dimensions for bathrooms. Spaced any closer together, the facilities would be difficult to use comfortably.

Planning a Bedroom

The most important factor (and sometimes the most difficult) in bedroom planning is the provision of an emergency exit. The code requires that every bedroom, including those in the basement, must have direct access to a door or a window that can be used in an emergency. The window must meet certain requirements, and the door must lead directly outdoors; it cannot lead to a bulkhead door.

Closets. The design and size of the closets in the bedroom depends in part on who is to use the room. A modestly sized closet probably suffices in a guest bedroom, but a master bedroom calls for a bigger one. Manufacturers of closet shelving and storage systems are good sources for closet-design information and can show how to pack the most storage into the least amount of space.

Planning a Recreation Room

The key to a great recreation room is versatility. Plan the space so that it can be used for a variety of activities. Wheeled storage cabinets, for example, can be rolled out of the way when hordes of 5-year-olds descend for a birthday party. Look for furniture that can be moved easily; build adaptable storage units; and install wall and floor surfaces that can stand up to the hard use this room typically sustains. Vinyl flooring, for example, is not stained by food spills (area rugs can give it "warmth") and wood paneling is more likely than drywall to survive chance encounters with cue sticks. An intense color or pattern can be overwhelming if used on all of the walls, but a spot of it (one brightly painted wall, for example) or some diagonal paneling can do wonders for a room. Wood paneling is a popular surface for recreation room walls because of its durability and visual warmth. In addition, the vertical lines of paneling create the illusion that the walls are taller than they are in reality.

There are no particular electrical requirements for the average recreation room, but the best plan is a versatile one. Make sure that there are plenty of receptacles for appliances like vacuums. Extra cable outlets provide the opportunity to place a TV in various locations and several phone jacks can be surprisingly convenient. Look closely at your family's interests, and plan for anything that might involve electricity, including lighted shelves for collectibles or outlets for fitness gear.

Planning a Shop

The solid floor and sturdy walls of a basement lend themselves nicely to the wear and tear that is typical of a wood shop. Because the height of the room is limited, however, additional horizontal space may be necessary to maneuver materials back and forth. Provide plenty of electrical outlets—they should be on a dedicated 20-amp circuit. Depending on the type of equipment used in the shop, 220v outlets as well as 110v outlets may be necessary. Given the proximity of the furnace and other combustion appliances (such as the water heater), and the lack of ventilation, it is not a good idea to work with stains and other wood finishing products in the confines of a basement shop.

Shop Lighting. Proper lighting is critical in a shop, so do not skimp on it. The ideal combination employs fluorescent lights for general lighting and incandescent lights for task and supplemental lighting. Wire the incandescents to one wall switch (because they hold up to being turned on and off frequently), and wire fluorescents to a second switch (to flip on only when you plan to be in the shop for a while). Fluorescent fixtures hung from short lengths of lightweight chain can be moved easily. Also, look for

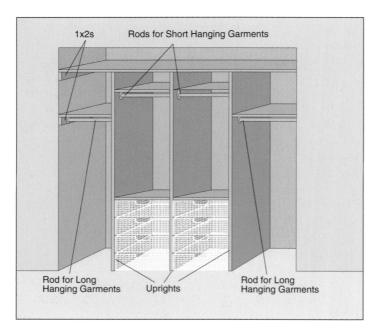

1x2s · Rods for Short Hanging Garments · Rod for Long Hanging Garments · Uprights · Rod for Long Hanging Garments

Closets. When planning for closets in your conversion, take stock of the items that you have and allow for long and short hanging garments. Install shelves and drawers to accommodate other clothing or things you want stored in the closet. These are the standard sizes of closets typically found in bedrooms. Note that the walk-in closet is a minimum 84 in. wide and the single closet is a minimum 48 in. wide.

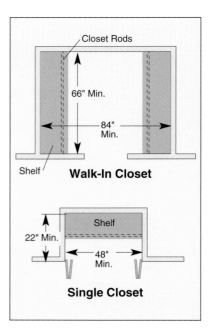

Closet Rods · 66" Min. · 84" Min. · Shelf · **Walk-In Closet** · Shelf · 22" Min. · 48" Min. · **Single Closet**

special break-resistant fluorescent and incandescent bulbs.

Dust Control. Keeping sawdust contained is another important precaution. Not only can dust be a nuisance when it ends up in living areas (or your lungs), but it also can play havoc with mechanical equipment. Furnaces call for special care. Dust quickly clogs the filters of a forced-air heating system, and even a boiler can be affected adversely by excessive dust. More importantly, however, excessive dust found near combustion appliances poses a fire hazard and under the right circumstances can even cause an explosion. (Keep a fire extinguisher handy.)

The best dust-control strategy is to use partition walls to isolate the shop from adjacent rooms. To keep dust where it belongs, treat each door that enters the shop as if it were an exterior door and weatherstrip it accordingly. A portable dust collection system connected to each machine cuts down the dust considerably, though it does not eliminate dust altogether. At the very least, connect a shop vacuum to each source of sawdust as the work is done.

Planning a Home Office

A home office is likely to be filled with electronic equipment that includes computers, printers, photocopiers, fax machines, and so on. Allow for plenty of electrical outlets, and as a precaution, divide them into at least two separate circuits if possible. Some pieces of home office equipment, such as laser printers, have significant power requirements, and if a circuit breaker trips while you're using the computer, you may lose important data.

Decide whether more than one telephone line is necessary for your home office. Convenience and organized record-keeping are other reasons to have two telephone lines. If one line is an extension of your home number and the other is for business only, you can answer personal calls without leaving the office and track business-call expenses separately.

Although it depends on the kind of work you'll do, most offices should have bookshelves, as well as storage for files, office supplies, and the like. Make every square foot count. If a tall four-drawer file cabinet seems too awkward for the room, for example, consider using a pair of two-drawer units with a piece of plywood on top. This arrangement allows for plenty of file space and serves as a stand

When planning a home office, don't forget to consider electrical requirements for computers, copiers, and other equipment.

for a printer, photocopier, fax machine, or work surface at the same time. Here are other factors to consider:

- **Separate Entrance.** Will you need direct access to the office to receive clients and accept deliveries?
- **Late Working Hours.** Will you work late at night? Will night work disrupt the sleep of other family members? For instance, don't combine a home office with a child's bedroom. Or if you set aside part of a master bedroom as an office, be sure late-night work won't disturb your spouse.
- **Home Office Tax Deductions.** Have you checked that you can legitimately declare the remodeled space as office space? Does your design conform to the regulations for home office space? Is it completely separated from other areas, for example, so 100 percent of the space is work related?
- **Insurance.** What liabilities will you incur if business guests must go through your living quarters to reach the office area? What about insuring your office equipment?
- **Zoning Ordinances.** Are there zoning restrictions that may influence your location of a home office?
- **Work at Home versus Occasional Use.** What is the purpose of the office now? How often will it be used? Do you need office space for two? Can the office be shared efficiently? Should you plan on using the home office full-time at some future date and incorporate anticipated needs with current design?

Planning a Home Theater

Media rooms are becoming increasingly popular. In addition to the electronic equipment, you will need comfortable seating, dedicated electrical service, and adjustable lighting. Plan seating in a home theater so that someone passing through the room won't have to walk between viewers and the video screen. Check that details such as electrical outlets and light switches are conveniently positioned if you've relocated doors. The electrical utilities should also relate to your prospective furniture arrangements. If you're planning a media wall with electrical demands, for instance, make sure the outlets are positioned to service it.

Home theaters and media rooms usually require extensive electrical work. Be sure to check the wiring requirements and the correct specifications for placing speakers with the equipment retailer.

Basic Clearance Requirements. Maintain the minimum clearances recommended here for the most comfortable use of doorways, furniture, and traffic areas.

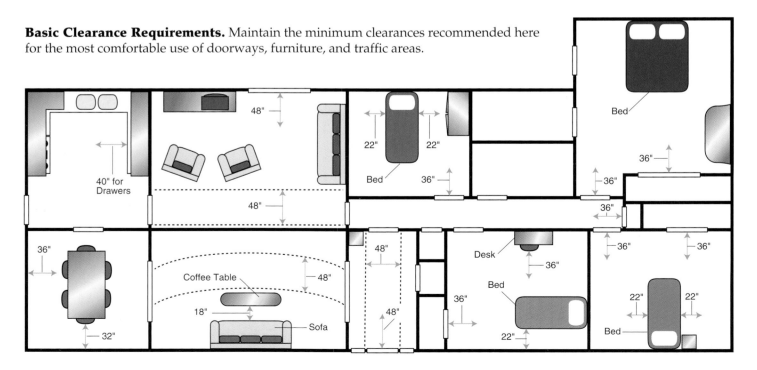

Lighting

To provide a suitable amount of natural light, building codes generally require that all habitable rooms have an amount of glazing (window glass area) equal to 8 percent or more of the floor area. For daylighting, it doesn't matter whether the glazing is fixed or operable. This amount of daylighting is difficult to achieve for rooms located partially below grade, so most building codes allow an exception to the requirement for these areas.

Natural lighting can be entirely forgone if artificial lighting provides an average of 6 lumens per square foot over the area of the room. Lumens are a measure of the total amount of light emitted by a light bulb; the more light a bulb produces, the higher its lumen rating. Six lumens per square foot is not difficult to achieve.

Note that the 6-lumen figure is for general, or ambient, lighting and is an average requirement for each room. The provision for general lighting is the first priority for planning room lighting. After that, task lighting and accent lighting can be added as desired. Special-purpose rooms like bathrooms and home offices may have additional lighting needs.

Designing with Light

To maximize the effectiveness of lighting, use light-colored surfaces wherever possible; this helps to reflect light around rooms. Dark paneling or carpeting, on the other hand, tends to "soak up" light. Use a variety of light sources, if possible, to provide maximum flexibility when it comes to setting a mood or producing extra light for activities.

Light Quality. Light quality is worth consideration, especially for basements. Even if the quantity of light is adequate, the quality of the light can make or break a room.

Lighting quality can be generally described in terms of the "coolness" or "warmth" of its color. This lighting temperature is measured using the Kelvin Scale, abbreviated K. Cool light emphasizes blue and green hues while warm light plays up yellows and reds. The color of the light you get depends on the kind of light bulb you use. Conventional fluorescent bulbs produce cool light while incandescent and halogen bulbs emit warm light. Because people tend to prefer warm light, they have traditionally avoided fluorescent lighting in homes. Modern fluorescent bulbs, however, are available in varieties that closely approximate the warmth of incandescent lighting. Look for fluorescent bulbs rated at less than 3000 K.

Lighting in Basement Conversions. Because you can't count on supplementary natural light, provide enough light to make the basement functional as well as attractive. You need ambient, overall lighting. In addition, you need task lighting, which puts a high level of illumination on the surfaces where you need it. In addition, make sure

Add light where you will need it. Think in terms of specific activity areas when designing a lighting system.

For basememt kitchens, be sure to include both ambient and task lighting in your design.

that there's adequate lighting for game tables and reading if these activities will take place in the basement. A basement's low light level makes it an ideal location for a media room or home entertainment center. You can totally control light levels and reduce glare without interference from the outdoors, as in aboveground installations.

Basic Fixture Types

Suspended. Globes, chandeliers, and other suspended fixtures can light a room or a table. Hang them 12 to 20 inches below an 8-foot ceiling or 30 to 36 inches above table height.

Surface-Mount. Attached directly to the ceiling, it distributes very even, shadowless general lighting. To minimize glare, surface-mount fixtures should be shielded. Fixtures with sockets for several smaller bulbs distribute more even lighting than those with just one or two large bulbs.

Recessed. Recessed fixtures, which mount flush with the ceiling or soffit, include fixed and aimable downlights, shielded fluorescent tubes, and totally luminous ceilings. Recessed fixtures require more wattage—up to twice as much as surface-mount and suspended types.

Track. Use a track system for general, task, or accent lighting—or any combination of the three. You can select from a broad array of modular fixtures, clip them anywhere along a track, and revise your lighting scheme any time you like. Locate tracks 12 to 24 inches out from the edges of wall cabinets to minimize shadows on counter-tops.

Under-Cabinet. Fluorescent or incandescent fixtures (with showcase bulbs) mounted to the undersides of wall cabinets bathe counters with efficient, inexpensive task lighting. Shield under-cabinet lights with valances and illuminate at least two-thirds of the counter's length.

Cove. Cove lights reflect upward to the ceiling, creating smooth, even general lighting or dramatic architectural effects. Consider locating custom cove lights on top of wall cabinets, in the space normally occupied by soffits.

How Much Light Do You Need?

TYPE	INCANDESCENT	FLUORESCENT	LOCATION
General (ambient) Lighting	2–4 watts per square foot of area. Double this if counters, cabinets, or flooring are dark	1–1½ watts per square foot of floor area	90 inches above the floor
Task Lighting			
Cleanup Centers	150 watts	30–40 watts	25 inches above the sink
Countertops	75–100 watts for each 3 running feet of work surface	20 watts for each 3 running feet of work surface	14–22 inches above the work surface
Cooking Centers	150 watts	30–40 watts	18–25 inches above burners. Most range hoods have lights.
Dining Tables	100–120 watts	Not applicable	25–30 inches above the table
Accent Lighting	Plan flexibility into accent lighting so that you can vary the mood with a flick of a switch or the twist of a dimmer. Suspended, recessed, track, and cove fixtures all work well.		

Assessing Potential Health Hazards

Every passing year seems to bring with it new warnings about possible health hazards in our homes. These should be taken seriously. The most common hazards are discussed below. For more information on these and other possible problems, visit the Web site of the U.S. Environmental Protection Agency (EPA) at www.epa.gov.

Carbon Monoxide. Carbon monoxide (CO) is produced by gas and kerosene heaters, fireplaces, wood stoves, furnaces, water heaters, gas stoves, cars, and other combustion devices. If it is not vented properly, carbon monoxide can build up in the home and cause serious injury (including death!) to the occupants. This can be a particular concern when remodeling a basement or garage. To ensure that no problems exist or are likely to be created once you start working, have a professional inspect all fuel-burning equipment and venting systems in your home and examine your remodeling plans. Install at least one CO detector in the remodeled space.

Radon. Radon is a colorless, odorless radioactive gas that comes from the natural breakdown of uranium in soil, rock, and water. When breathed into the body, molecules of radon lodge in the lungs and lead to an increased risk of lung cancer. Radon typically moves up through the ground and into a house through cracks and holes in the foundation, though they are not the only source. Because radon tends to concentrate in room closest to the ground, it's particularly important to test for the gas before converting a basement or garage to living space. If test results indicate that there's a problem, radon-reduction techniques are relatively easy to incorporate into remodeling plans.

There are two basic ways to test for radon. Short-term tests use small monitors, such as charcoal canisters, that remain in your home for two days to three months, depending on the monitor. Long-term tests use detectors that remain in your home for more than three months. A long-term test usually offers a better guide to the average radon level in your home throughout the year.

A reading of 1.3 picocuries per liter of air (pc/l) is considered normal. If testing indicates a level of more than 4 pc/l, take steps to reduce radon through mitigation. Levels less than 4 pc/l are usually not worth the cost of mitigation.

Sealing cracks and other openings in the foundation is a basic part of most radon-reduction approaches, but the EPA does not consider sealing alone to be effective.

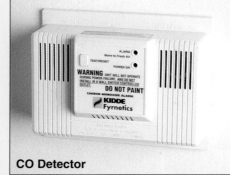

CO Detector

In most cases, reduction systems that incorporate pipes and fans to vent air to the outdoors are preferred. Check with a licensed mitigation expert.

Asbestos. Asbestos is a fibrous mineral found in rocks and soil. Alone or in combination with other materials, asbestos was once fashioned into a variety of building materials because it is a strong, durable fire retardant and an efficient insulator. Unfortunately, it's also a carcinogen. Once inhaled, asbestos fibers lodge in the lungs. Because the material is so durable, it remains in the lung tissue and becomes concentrated as repeated exposure occurs over time. Asbestos can cause cancer of the lungs and stomach among those who have prolonged work-related exposure to it. Home health risks arise when age, accidental damage, normal cleaning, or remodeling activities cause the asbestos-containing materials to crumble, flake, or deteriorate. According to the EPA, houses constructed in the United States since 1970 are less likely to contain asbestos products than those built before that time. Asbestos is sometimes found around pipes, furnaces, ductwork, and beams, and in some vinyl flooring materials, ceiling tiles, exterior roofing, and wallboard products.

If you suspect that asbestos may be present in your house, have the area inspected by a professional before remodeling. Undamaged asbestos-containing material can usually be left alone as long as remodeling nearby will not disturb it. Never attempt to remove asbestos yourself.

Lead. If your house was built before 1979, there is a good chance that the paint used on it contains lead. If your remodeling plans call for any need to scrape, sand, or remove painted surfaces, first determine whether there is lead in the paint. Your public health department should be able to tell you how to test the paint and what to do if lead is found in it.

Mold. Moist air, such as is found in many basements, can allow mold to thrive. Small amounts of mold can stain surfaces and cause unpleasant odors, while larger concentrations can trigger allergic reactions, asthma, and other respiratory problems. If mold is a problem, the first thing to do is get rid of the moisture that is allowing it to flourish. Reduce the indoor humidity to less than 60 percent through ventilation, air conditioning, dehumidifiers, and exhaust fans. Minimize condensation with insulation. Remove and discard all moldy materials and wash surfaces using a 50-50 solution of water and bleach.

Planning for Utilities

Converting a basement into usable living space almost always requires that you arrange for expanded heating and cooling as well as new electrical wiring. It also often entails an extension of the plumbing system. These features can often be the most difficult and expensive components of a remodel, so be sure to plan thoroughly before beginning any work.

Planning the HVAC System

As part of a preconstruction review of your basement conversion, give some thought to how these spaces will be heated and cooled. Though it might seem tempting simply to hope that the heated space above a basement will somehow share the warmth or that the earth surrounding a basement act as a natural insulator, neither will work. Fortunately, your home's existing HVAC system can usually be extended to the basement if you have forced-air heating and cooling, electric baseboard heat, or hydronic (hot water) heat.

In many cases, an electric baseboard or fan-forced electric heater is enough to supply all the necessary heat for a modest-size rooms in a large basement as long as you supply a heater for each room. However, this can become expensive and will look intrusive. Electric baseboard and fan-forced wall-mounted heaters can be installed in home conversions regardless of the kind of heating system that already exists in the rest of the house. The electric service panel, however, must be able to accommodate the additional load. A direct-vent space heater fueled by natural gas, propane, or kerosene can also be a good option for conversions. Contact a heating contractor for advice before applying for a building permit. He or she will be able to suggest a suitable heater type and size and make recommendations with regard to routing heating ducts or pipes before new flooring, walls, and ceilings are installed in your new living area.

Planning the Electrical System

Although it's possible to extend an existing electrical circuit to a basement, doing so may overload the circuit. Extending a circuit that already exists doesn't provide enough power for most conversions. Plan to run at

least one new circuit to a basement conversion. Although most basements probably already have at least one circuit, it's best to add one or two to ensure against overloading. If you're building a home office in the basement, plan to add two or more circuits and remember to have telecommunications lines installed.

Electric heaters must be served by a separate circuit. All electrical circuits in basements must meet the same electrical code requirements that govern other living spaces in the house. To accommodate the added electrical load, service to the house must be at least 100 amperes. If your house has 200-ampere service, as most newer homes do, adding the new circuits is easy. Newer homes also have three-wire service. Most homes built before 1941 that have not been upgraded have two-wire electric service, which may limit the number and type of electrical appliances that can be used. Consult a licensed electrician to determine whether the current system can be added to, modified, or upgraded.

Recessed wall heaters. These units provide spot heating to relatively small spaces. They operate by a thermostat or a timer.

Electric baseboard heaters. These systems add heat to individual rooms. You may need to run a new electrical circuit to power the baseboard heater.

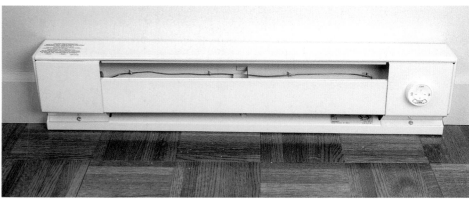

Planning the Plumbing System

Supplying cold water to a new space is usually an easy task. Hot water can be trickier, and the DWV (drain, waste, and vent) system can be a headache, especially in the basement or garage.

Hot-Water Supply. If your water comes from a well, the ability of the system to support a new bathroom is subject to the capacity of the pump and well. Because the water heater is probably sized to the existing house, you might want to add a point-of-use tankless water heater.

DWV System. Draining wastewater and sewage is accomplished through a network of pipes that leads to the sewer or septic tank. For these pipes to drain freely, they must be connected to a system of vent pipes that leads up to and through the roof.

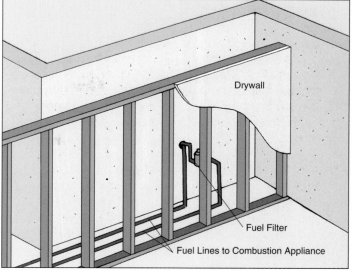

Drywall

Fuel Filter

Fuel Lines to Combustion Appliance

Service Corridors. To reach equipment that needs periodic maintenance, such as filters, leave about 24 in. of space between a foundation wall and a partition.

Whole-House Drain and Vent Systems

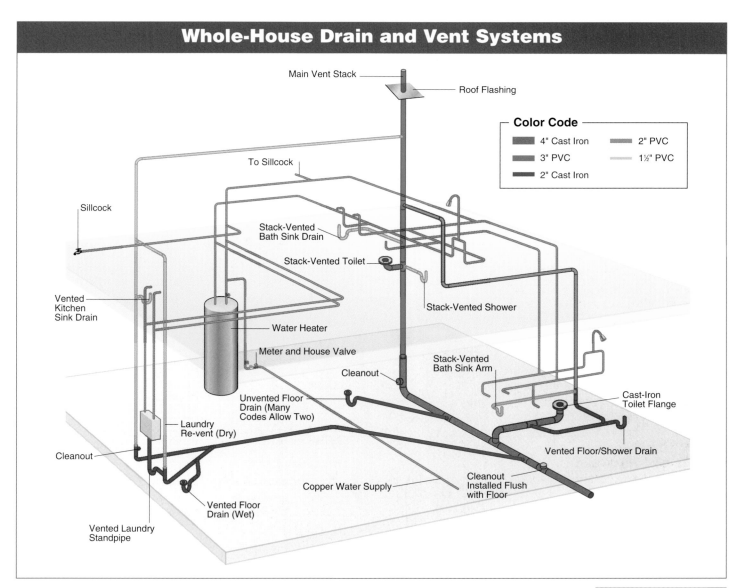

Main Vent Stack

Roof Flashing

Color Code

4" Cast Iron		2" PVC
3" PVC		1½" PVC
2" Cast Iron		

To Sillcock

Sillcock

Stack-Vented Bath Sink Drain

Stack-Vented Toilet

Stack-Vented Shower

Vented Kitchen Sink Drain

Water Heater

Meter and House Valve

Cleanout

Stack-Vented Bath Sink Arm

Cast-Iron Toilet Flange

Unvented Floor Drain (Many Codes Allow Two)

Laundry Re-vent (Dry)

Vented Floor/Shower Drain

Cleanout

Copper Water Supply

Cleanout Installed Flush with Floor

Vented Floor Drain (Wet)

Vented Laundry Standpipe

Building codes specify the width as well as the tread depth and riser height for stairs.

Abiding by Building Codes

Building regulations have been around since at least 2000 B.C., when the Code of Hammurabi mandated death to the son of a builder whose building collapsed and killed the son of its owner. Codes these days are not so severe, but they do have something in common with their predecessor in that they reflect the fundamental duty of government to protect the general health, safety, and welfare of its citizens.

Knowing the Codes

The codes in your community might cover everything from the way the house is used to the materials you can use for building or remodeling it. Other communities may have adopted some types of fire codes, accessibility codes (requiring barrier-free access to buildings), or special construction codes, such as those requiring earthquake-resistance construction. Contact your local building department to learn the combination of codes that applies to your area.

Building Code. Building codes cover such things as the suitability of construction materials, the span of floor joists, the amount of insulation needed in a ceiling, the kind and number of fasteners used to fasten sheathing, and the amount of light and ventilation necessary to provide a healthy living space. Building codes also cover some aspects of plumbing and wiring installations.

Mechanical Code. The installation of heating and cooling equipment (including ducts), woodstoves, and chimneys is covered by mechanical codes.

Plumbing Code. Plumbing codes cover water-supply and drain, waste, and vent (DWV) systems.

Energy Codes. In response to energy shortages in the 1970s, many municipalities instituted codes that map out minimum requirements for window glazing, insulation, and general energy efficiency. Some energy codes include the use of energy-efficient appliances so be sure to check requirements in your area.

Electrical Code. The National Electrical Code applies to the entire country. The code covers the proper installation of household electrical equipment and wiring systems.

Who Will Do the Work?

If you want someone else to do all of the work, including locating and negotiating with each specialty contractor, hire a builder or general contractor. A builder generally works with his or her own team of specialists, while a general contractor works with various independent subcontractors. You may choose to take on the role of general contractor. That means the job of hiring each subcontractor is in your hands. Working as the general contractor may save money but can be surprisingly time consuming.

Getting Bids. Screen all potential contractors before hiring them to work on your house. Ask for references, and call several people for whom he or she recently worked. The larger the job, the more important

it is to shop around. Get at least three bids for every phase of work. Keep in mind that the lowest bid is not always the best deal. Make sure that the professional can do the job when and how you want it, and be sure to get all agreements in writing. Provide a simple set of plans or sketches to all bidders, including each type and grade of material required, to ensure that all parties understand exactly what the job entails and can bid accordingly.

During construction, you might decide to make some changes. If so, talk to the contractor and come to an agreement on the cost of the change. Then put it in writing. This is called a change order, and it helps to prevent misunderstandings later.

Following the Codes

For many years, three building-code organizations existed in the United States, each one promoting its own "model code" over a specific region of the country. This created standards and requirements that often varied considerably from one area to another. Fortunately, the three groups have established a single organization, the International Code Council (ICC), whose goal is to produce a single set of codes for the entire country. The International Codes (or I-Codes) are slowly but surely being adopted by states and jurisdictions throughout the country.

Until such time as the I-Codes become universally adopted and uniformly implemented, local codes will continue to exercise significant influence over building practices. Before you begin any building projects, it is wise to investigate your own local code requirements.

City or Town Level. Check with the local building and zoning department, if there is one, or with the housing department or town clerk.

County Level. If you live outside the boundaries of a city or town, check with the county clerk or county commission.

State Level. If you can't find a city or county office that covers building codes, check with the state offices. Codes may be administered by the departments of housing, community affairs, or building standards, or even by the labor department.

Do You Need a Permit? Permits and inspections are a way of enforcing the building codes. Essentially, a permit is the license that gives you permission to do the work, and an inspection ensures that you did the work according to code. Usually a permit is not necessary for minor repair or remodeling work, but you may need one for adding a dormer, extending the water supply and DWV system, or adding an electrical circuit. You almost always need one to convert a basement into living space.

Inspections. When a permit is required, a city or county building inspector has to examine the work. He or she checks to see that the work meets or exceeds the building codes. With small projects, an inspector might require only a final inspection; with a larger project, several inspections may be necessary. In any case, it's your responsibility to arrange for the inspection.

Zoning Ordinances. Another kind of regulation that can affect your project is called a zoning ordinance. Some residential zoning ordinances are designed to keep multifamily homes out of single-family neighborhoods. If your basement conversion plans call for the addition of a small bathroom and a separate outside entrance, local zoning officials might interpret this as an attempt to add a rental unit and may deny a permit. You will need to change your plans to obtain a permit. Zoning ordinances sometimes restrict the height of a house or your ability to change its exterior. If you want to add bedrooms, zoning ordinances might require you to enlarge your septic system. Another bedroom implies another resident, which in turn implies increased demand on the septic system. Though most basement conversions don't run afoul of zoning ordinances, it's always a good idea to check with local officials before doing any work.

Obtaining a Permit

Depending on the scope of the work, a permit application will include the following items:

- **A Legal Description of the Property.** You can get this from city or county records or directly from your deed.
- **A Drawing of Proposed Changes.** This drawing need not be done by an architect but must clearly show the structural changes you plan to make. It must also identify the type and dimension of all materials. Most building departments accept basement conversion plans drawn by a homeowner as long as the details are clearly labeled. Large projects may require drawings from an architect. Note the dimensions and span of existing and new materials.
- **A Site Plan Drawing.** This shows the position of the house on the lot and the approximate location of adjacent houses. It also shows the location of the well and septic system, if any.

Room Sizes

The table below shows the minimum sizes of rooms in feet as set forth by the U. S. Department of Housing and Urban Development.

Room	HUD Minimum	Preferred Minimum
Living room	11 x 16	12 x 18
Family room/Den	10½ x 10½	12 x 16
Great room	—	14 x 20
Kitchen*	—	—
Master bedroom	—	12 x 16
Other bedrooms	8 x 10	11 x 14
Bathroom (full)	5 x 7	5 x 9

*The size of the kitchen will vary with the selection of cabinets and the appliance layout.

chapter 2

room prep

Surveying the Basement

Once you have an idea of how you want to remodel the basement, a bit of detective work is necessary. Uncovering and solving potential problems at the start means being faced with fewer surprises and less expense later.

Not every basement can be converted into living space, and not every one that can is worth the effort. If, for example, the basement is short on headroom, the solution (lowering the floor level) involves more effort and expense than it's worth. Likewise, if water problems can't be eliminated despite your best efforts, you can't turn the basement into a comfortable and healthy living space. Spend some time getting to know your basement before jumping into a remodeling job.

Types of Basement Walls

The kind and condition of the walls found in the basement have a lot to do with how easy or hard the basement will be to remodel. Basement walls, of course, are the inside surfaces of the foundation. They can be made of concrete block, poured concrete, stone, or pressure-treated wood. Though some are easier to work with than others, none of the foundation types automatically prevent you from remodeling the basement. It's easy, for example, to install drywall or paneling on the walls of a pressure-treated wood foundation. The procedure is the same for installing drywall on wood-framed walls. A stone foundation, on the other hand, sometimes has water problems that are difficult to remedy due to the irregular nature of the materials. Walls of concrete block or poured concrete are the most common.

Concrete-Block Walls. A foundation made with concrete blocks is easy to identify because of the grid pattern created by horizontal and vertical mortar joints. Each block has a hollow core, and the inside and outside faces of the block are connected by integral webs. The hollow structure of the block makes it lightweight and easy to work with and allows the wall to be strengthened by mortaring reinforcing bar, or rebar, into the cores.

Blocks are stacked one atop the other. Mortar placed between each row and each block bonds the units and results in a strong, solid wall. Because of this construction method, the ultimate strength and water-resistance of the basement wall depends on both the condition of the blocks and the condition of the mortar.

Poured-Concrete Walls. A poured-concrete wall is monolithic and has a smooth surface. To build such a wall, concrete (a mixture of sand, gravel, water, and portland cement) is poured into form work, usually made from steel or some other metal. Steel reinforcing bars are placed in the forms prior to the pour. The bars strengthen a concrete wall and help resist cracking.

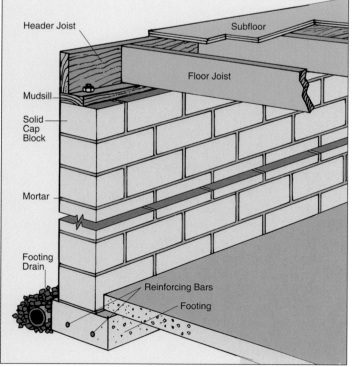

Concrete-Block Walls. This system consists of individual blocks bonded together with mortar. The block size shown here is the most common.

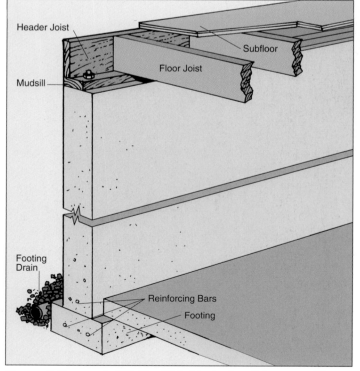

Poured Concrete Walls. This kind of wall is poured from footing to top, often in one step. Steel reinforcing bars are added for additional strength.

Other Types of Walls. In some areas of the country, particularly the Midwest, builders may frame a house on top of a foundation of 2x8 or larger studs and plates that have been treated with chemicals under pressure to resist decay. This is a relatively new type of foundation. Sheathed on the outside with pressure-treated plywood and detailed carefully to eliminate water infiltration, the foundation can be insulated and finished like a standard framed wall.

Stone foundations can still be found in certain areas of the country, such as the Northeast, where some houses predate the availability of concrete. Although the kind of stone varies according to that which was available locally, most of the foundations were laid up with mortar. To find out whether the foundation is in good condition, it's worth having a mason inspect it before remodeling the basement.

Inspecting the Basement

Before beginning work, there's more you must know about your basement. It's easier to deal with a tricky basement problem before a small mountain of building materials is delivered to the front yard rather than after.

Inadequate Headroom. According to most building codes, a room in the basement must have a minimum ceiling height of 90 inches over at least one-half of the room. The only exceptions are bathrooms, kitchens, and hallways, which are allowed a ceiling height of 84 inches.

Exit Strategies. According to code, all bedrooms in the basement must have a means of emergency exit. A door that leads directly to the outside from a bedroom (and not to a bulkhead door) qualifies as an emergency exit. If no such door exists, there must be an egress window that has 5.7 square feet of operable area. If remodeling plans include a bedroom, make the egress issue the first order of business.

Sagging Joists. Sight across the underside of the floor joists to see whether they are out of line. Those that are out of line probably are damaged but most likely can be repaired.

Moisture Problems. Of all the possible roadblocks to making the basement livable, moisture problems can be the toughest to hurdle. Water is incredibly persistent,

and under some circumstances can make its way through walls that are considered impermeable. Another source of moisture is the condensation that forms as warm moist air reaches the cold surface of a masonry wall. To check for moisture problems, perform the simple test described in "Moisture Problems," opposite.

Insect Problems. Check the outer 12 inches or so of the floor joists, the inside surface of the rim and header joists, and the wood frame of every basement window. Keep an eye out for signs of powder-post beetles, carpenter ants, and non-subterranean termites. Signs of insect problems include swarming insects, a series of pinholes in the wood, and small powdery piles of sawdust beneath affected wood. To search for rot or insect damage, use the tip of a screwdriver or awl to poke at the rim and header joists, the plate, the ends of the joists, and window framing, even if the wood looks sound. Rotten or insect-infested wood yields easily. Infested areas must be treated by a professional exterminator.

Foundation Cracks. Figuring out what to do about foundation cracks is more art than science. Hairline cracks in a concrete wall are sometimes the fault of improper curing; larger cracks are usually due to settling. Both kinds can be repaired with hydraulic cement if the crack isn't an active one, that is, if whatever caused the crack in the first place is no longer an existing problem. If the foundation is in the process of settling, however, or if some other factor is stressing the foundation, cracks you patch today may open again tomorrow.

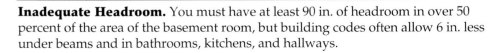

Inadequate Headroom. You must have at least 90 in. of headroom in over 50 percent of the area of the basement room, but building codes often allow 6 in. less under beams and in bathrooms, kitchens, and hallways.

Sagging Joists. Sight across the underside of the joists to spot those that are out of line. Then check to see whether the whole floor system is sagging.

Moisture Problems. Tape aluminum foil to sections of the basement or garage floor and foundation walls. If moisture collects underneath, a seepage problem exists and must be corrected; if it's on top, a humidity problem exists. (See also page 25.)

Insect Problems. Inspect the joists and other wood in the basement for dry rot and insects. Use an awl to penetrate the outer joist areas.

Repairing Joists

The ceiling joists not only support the floor above the basement, they will also provide the base for any finished ceiling you want to add to your new basement living area, so they should be even across the basement ceiling. You can check to determine if the joists are level by placing a 4-foot level across several joists. If they are not even, the level will rock over the area that is sagging. To repair a weak joist, prop up the sagging joist and reinforce it by installing a new joist next to the sagging one—a process called "sistering." Use lumber of the same size as the original joist, and attach the new framing to the old using construction adhesive and screws.

Locate a weak or sagging joist by checking across several joists using a level. It will rock over the lowest one where the joist dips.

Strengthen a weak joist (after propping it up if need be) by adding a second joist secured with construction adhesive and screws.

Planning the Logistics

Turning your basement into livable space calls for a surprisingly large volume of materials and introduces some unusual logistical issues. Even small projects require flooring, lengths of baseboard, sheets of drywall, and buckets of joint compound. Getting all of these materials into the basement can be tricky.

Basement

If your plans call for installing windows in a basement that has no exterior door, have the openings cut out before starting the rest of the renovation. A concrete-cutting company will have to be hired for this work. Once the window openings are made and reinforced, leave them open until all materials have been delivered through them and into the basement area. Rough openings can be temporarily secured with plywood nailed over them.

Lumber Transport. If your project requires support beams, joists, and posts, it probably needs them in unwieldy lengths. The most direct route isn't always the best when you're carrying 12-foot 2x8s. Look for the route that has the fewest turns.

Subflooring, Paneling, and Drywall Transport. Plywood, drywall, and other sheet goods usually come in 4 x 8-foot sheets. This makes them awkward to carry through the house, particularly down the stairs. Cut plywood on the ground, if possible, to fit as needed—for example, if your project calls for short knee walls. Subflooring and drywall panels are used full size, however, to maintain their structural integrity or for efficiency.

If you need a lot of panels, transport them in small groups over a period of several days, and install each group before bringing in the next one. This doesn't save you time, but it reduces back strain and minimizes congestion at the work site.

Tub-and-Shower Unit Transport. Depending on your project, you might be able to simply carry a new tub or shower down the stairs into the basement. If you have a walk-out basement, you should be able to carry all but the very largest tubs through the door opening. Fortunately, the weight of the tub usually isn't a concern during a basement remodeling. Consider tiling the surround if you can't get a one-piece unit into the basement. You may also choose to use one of the tub-surround kits designed for remodeling work.

Store drywall where it is protected from the elements. Place stacks close to where they will be installed.

Drywall Transport. Use a metal lifting hook to help carry sheets of drywall or plywood.

Wall Removal

Nearly every remodeling project calls for the removal of existing walls or surfaces before the rest of the work can begin. Sometimes, a wall in the basement must be removed to make room for a new stairway. Old partition walls in a basement may need to be removed to open up the space for a new recreation room. Although most unfinished basements are generally free of extra walls, previous owners may have enclosed a small section for a darkroom, hobby area, or shop.

Putting a house together can be hazardous, but taking one apart, even partially, calls for particular vigilance. Many accidents occur simply because people expect demolition to be easy. It's not. Be as careful as you would be with any other construction project. In addition to the general safety tips listed at the front of this book, pay particular attention to the guidelines under "Demolition Safety."

Removing Drywall

Electrical wire can generally be fished through walls, floors, and ceilings with a minimal need to remove sections of drywall or plaster to gain access around framing members. Running plumbing pipes, on the other hand, will require the removal of drywall or plaster because plumbing is bulkier. Many times, especially with large projects, you're best off removing all the drywall or plaster on a wall to obtain clear and unobstructed access to the wall cavities.

In some cases, you might only have to remove drywall or plaster along the bottom 24 or 36 inches of a wall to gain access for electrical wiring and plumbing pipes. The most common indoor wall surface is ½-inch-thick drywall. The material itself isn't particularly tough, but the number of nails or screws used to attach it make it awkward and messy to remove.

Bang a starter hole through the old drywall using the claw of a hammer or with a pry bar tapped with the hammer. Use the claw of the hammer or pry bar to pull off a large chunk at a time, removing all nails as you go. Protect your hands with gloves when removing metal trim edges.

SMART TIP

Develop a plan before you start demolition. Before you pick up a pry bar, know how you will safely dispose of the materials you remove. Check with the local building department for requirements. Check lead times for any special-order items you may need. Nothing is more frustrating than stopping work while you wait for an item to be delivered.

Demolition Safety

- Wear work boots and pants. Not only do work boots help protect your feet from debris, they also shield your ankles from the scrapes and cuts commonly caused by demolition work. Wear long pants to protect your legs.
- Wear leather work gloves. Gloves that have cuffs to protect your wrists are best. Canvas gloves can be pierced easily and are not good for this type of work.
- Wear a dust mask, and change it frequently. Even a small amount of demolition kicks up a lot of dust.
- Always wear safety glasses—particularly when using power tools or a hammer.
- Remove nails promptly. Taking nails out of pieces of wood or pounding them flat as you remove the wood itself prevents you from stepping on them as you progress with the work.
- Frequently clean up the area, and remove excess debris.
- Proceed methodically. Remove materials piece by piece and layer by layer.
- Never remove a wall until you know whether it's a bearing wall. Always assume that there's wiring or plumbing in the wall even if it's not evident.
- Be careful around materials suspected of containing asbestos. The repair or removal of products that contain asbestos must be done by a trained contractor. The local building deparment can supply more information.

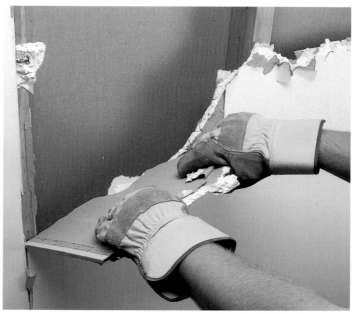

Remove drywall in large sections. Be sure to check for plumbing, wiring, and ducting before cutting into a wall.

Removing Plaster and Lath

Stripping plaster from a wall is dirty work no matter how it's done. Some people prefer to cut it away in chunks using a circular saw with a masonry blade set to make a shallow cut. Others find it easier just to batter the plaster with a hammer, pull it away in chunks, and pry away the lath using a wrecking bar. In either case, be certain to wear safety goggles and a good-quality dust mask.

Removing Framing

There are two basic types of walls in every house, and it's essential that you identify each one before attempting to remove it. If you skip this step, you risk injury to yourself and serious damage to your house.

Bearing Walls. A wall that supports structural loads, such as a floor, a roof, or another wall above, and helps to transmit those loads to the foundation of the house is a bearing wall. Except for gable end walls, exterior walls are usually bearing walls. Walls that run lengthwise through the center of a house are normally bearing walls. Joists that run along each side of the house rest on the center bearing wall. Bearing walls sometimes can be spotted from the attic. Look for two sets of overlapping joists. The wall on which the ends rest is a bearing wall.

You also may be able to identify bearing walls from the basement. Look for walls that rest atop a beam or a basement wall. If you're not sure about the kind of wall you're dealing with, the safest thing is to assume that it's a bearing wall. Seek professional advice from a builder or engineer when you must remove a bearing wall.

Nonbearing Walls. Nonbearing walls, also called partition walls, support only the wall covering attached to them. It is usually safe to remove a nonbearing wall. If a wall doesn't support joist ends and doesn't lie directly beneath a post, it may be a nonbearing wall.

Wiring and Plumbing. Before removing a wall, check the area immediately above and beneath it from the attic and basement. Look for wires, pipes, or ducts that lead into the wall. There's no way to tell for sure how big the job is until you pull the drywall or plaster from at least one side of the wall.

Wiring is easy to relocate, but water supply piping is more difficult. Plumbing vent pipes are trickier still, primarily because of code requirements that restrict their placement. Heating ducts and drainpipes are the toughest of all to relocate. Consult a professional if you're unsure of what to do.

Removing a Stud Wall

When you find one or two studs that are throwing the wall out of kilter or studs damaged by rot, replace them. Because wall studs are nailed through horizontal pieces at the top and bottom of the wall, you can't get at these nails to pull them. The most practical plan is to cut the stud you want to remove in half and pry out the pieces one at a time. If you are replacing several studs in a load-bearing wall, the safest approach is to install one or two temporary braces until the new studs are in place.

Trimming Nails. Where sharp nails remain in the top and bottom frame of the wall, slice them off flush using a hacksaw or reciprocating saw fitted with a metal-cutting blade.

1. Use a reciprocating saw or a saber saw to start cutting through the damaged stud about halfway up the wall. Stay clear of pipes or wires.

2. To keep the stud from binding on the saw blade (even if you cut by hand) insert a wedge to keep the cut open as you complete the job.

3. Once you cut through, pry out the stud in two pieces. Remember to trim the nails driven through the top and bottom of the wall frame.

Cleaning Masonry Block

There are several ways to clean masonry. Most of the methods apply to brick, concrete, and stone as well as to block. Many of the more complicated methods are generally handled by contractors, including sandblasting and cleaning with chemicals or steam. Another option, cleaning with a pressure-washer, is a job that most do-it-yourselfers can handle.

Sandblasting takes away surface and embedded dirt. Chemical- and steam-cleaning contractors can solve a variety of problems, including removing efflorescence, which is a powdery crust. (See "How Efflorescence Forms," below.)

Mold and mildew also may take hold on masonry that is not exposed to sunlight. To test a discolored patch of block wall, drop a small amount of bleach on the spot. The bleach will whiten mildew growth but will have no effect on dirt. To clear the mildew, scrub the area with a solution of one part bleach to one part warm water, and then rinse.

Remove stains from iron hardware by applying a solution of oxalic acid. Mix about 1 pound of the crystals in a gallon of water with ½ pound of ammonium bifluoride; brush the mix over the stained area; and then rinse.

How Efflorescence Forms

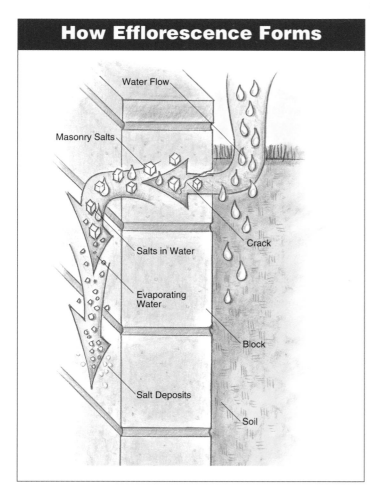

Water Flow

Masonry Salts

Salts in Water

Crack

Evaporating Water

Block

Salt Deposits

Soil

Foil Test for Wet Basements

Water leaking through a crack in a foundation is usually easy to detect. But basement walls also can become wet due to excessive moisture in the air that condenses on the masonry, particularly in the summer. To determine whether you have a leak or a condensation problem, tape down a patch of aluminum foil, which moisture can't penetrate, over a section of clean, dry wall (top). Check for moisture after 48 hours. If the foil surface is wet but the wall below it is dry (middle), the problem is condensation. If the foil surface is dry but the wall beneath it is wet (bottom), then the problem is water seeping through the wall.

Moisture Problems

Moisture problems can be an issue in just about any part of the house, but they are particularly common in basements. If moisture is finding its way into the space you plan to remodel, seasonally or routinely, don't think that you can simply cover up the problem area with a new surface. Instead, find the source of the moisture infiltration and fix it before remodeling.

Eliminating Basement Moisture Problems

A basement with large foundation walls, can't be turned into a suitable living space unless it's guaranteed to stay dry. Water problems range in seriousness from mild condensation and seepage to periodic flooding. Given enough time and money, most water problems can be solved. But that doesn't mean the effort is justified. Assuming that the plumbing doesn't leak, basement moisture comes from either seepage (water from outside the house leaking through walls or floor) or condensation (the result of warm moist air hitting a cold masonry wall or cold water pipes). The source of the water problem can be identified by performing a simple test. (See "Foil Test for Wet Basements," page 25.)

Condensation. If condensation is the problem, eliminate it either by installing a portable dehumidifier in the basement or by insulating the walls and water pipes.

Sealing Walls

For minor moisture problem, apply a coat of masonry waterproofer to the inside walls of the basement. These products can provide protection against minor seepage through concrete and concrete-block walls. However, major water problems require more drastic measures. The sealers go by the names waterproofing paint, basement paint, or basement waterproofer.

Brush the sealer on the walls. Work it into the surface of the concrete block.

Dealing with moisture is a common problem with remodeling a basement. Many problems can be solved through exterior drainage and proper grading around the house.

Seepage. Seepage water is more difficult to eliminate because it might be coming from any or all of the following sources:

- **Gutter Systems.** Leaders that dump water near the foundation encourage water to soak in at exactly the wrong places. Use splash blocks or leader extensions to direct water away from the house.
- **Improper Grading.** To conduct water away from the foundation, the grade must drop at least 2½ to 6 inches in 10 feet all around the house. Fill in pockets that encourage water to pool.
- **Lack of Footing Drains.** Some water inevitably reaches the bottom of the foundation, but it will not be a problem if perforated pipes, called footing drains, lead it away. Most newer houses have footing drains, but older homes may not. Drains can be added to older houses, though not without considerable effort. This is a job for a contractor.
- **Cracked Foundation Walls.** Water finds a way to get through even the smallest cracks, so use hydraulic cement to patch them.
- **Pipes or Electrical Lines.** Seal gaps around pipes with hydraulic cement or silicone sealant.
- **High Water Table.** The water table varies in depth from area to area and even from season to season. Nothing can be done about the level, but foundation drains and sump pumps help conduct water away.

Correcting Severe Water Problems

If water continues to enter the basement despite efforts to seal the walls from the inside, the problem must be tackled from the outside. If excessive quantities of water build up in the soil just outside the foundation, they will be forced (by hydrostatic pressure) through the masonry. Water that's under a modest amount of pressure can be sealed out with waterproofing paint; however, large amounts of pressure can defeat any product that's applied to the inside of a wall. A waterproofing layer applied to the outside of the foundation is far more effective.

Exterior Waterproofing. The more pressure applied to an exterior waterproofing coating, the tighter the waterproofing adheres to the wall. It's not easy to waterproof the outside of the foundation, however, and it can be quite expensive. Because all possible strategies involve a good bit of excavation, this work is best left to a contractor. Compare several estimates before signing a contract. And be sure to deal with a firm that has experience in this area.

Sump Pumps. One fairly easy way to keep the basement dry is to install an electric sump pump, which draws water from beneath the slab and pumps it away from the house. The pump sits in a hole, or sump, that extends below the slab. A sump pump may be part of a larger strategy to keep water out.

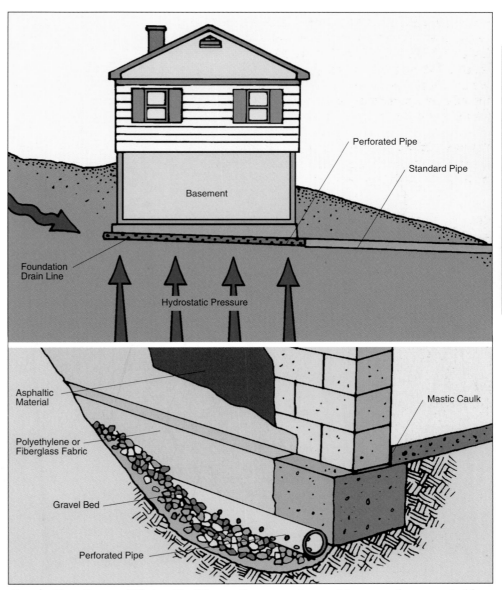

Correcting Severe Water Problems. Severe water problems can be corrected by intercepting water before it reaches the foundation with foundation drains.

Diagnosing Cracks

Minor cracks in block walls generally are nothing to worry about as long as the cracks are stable. (You'll often see debris or old paint in stable cracks.) Larger cracks that appear suddenly or keep expanding could signal a serious structural flaw, particularly if the crack extends in a staircase pattern through several courses of block. To track a new crack, tape gridded tracing paper over the area, outline the crack, and measure its length and widest parts. Mark the corners of the tracing paper on the wall so that you can reposition the paper exactly as you placed it the first time in order to see if the crack changes over time.

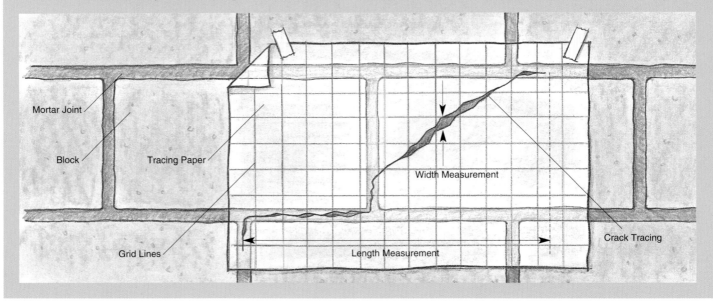

Mortar Joint
Block
Tracing Paper
Grid Lines
Width Measurement
Length Measurement
Crack Tracing

Drying Out Basements

Water can leak into basements through cracks or mortar joints in the foundation walls. But there is another common cause of basement moisture: condensation, which forms when water vapor in warm air hits the cool foundation walls.

Leaks can usually be identified by sight and repaired with hydraulic cement. This dense patch material swells as it hardens and can be used on wet cracks and active leaks. The foil test shown on page 25 will help you decide whether moisture is due to a leak in the walls or condensation problems.

Solve condensation problems by improving ventilation and using air conditioners and dehumidifiers. Eliminating seepage, however, is another matter. If seepage occurs only during heavy rains, the solution could be as simple as extending a downspout so that the runoff is directed farther away from foundation walls or regrading the soil so that it slopes away from the foundation.

Correct minor seepage from the inside by coating foundation walls with a masonry sealer (either a cement- or tar-based product or a waterproof silicone sealer). As a last (and very expensive) resort, you may need to re-excavate the foundation down to the footings to install perimeter drains and to apply new waterproofing.

Making Repairs

To keep basement moisture and leaks from turning into major problems, inspect basement walls on a regular basis, especially after heavy rains. In addition to checking for cracks and holes, look for moisture penetration through the mortar joints in concrete blocks and floor-to-wall joints. Also look for gaps around windows, doors, and vents, such as dryer vents. If your basement takes on water after a rain, try to determine its source so that you can make necessary repairs.

Repair holes and cracks as soon as you discover them, but bear in mind that filling a crack takes care of the symptom, not the underlying cause. A large amount of water entering a basement is a sign of a drainage problem that is best dealt with outside of the house—for instance, by installing an area drain.

Small to moderate-size cracks that are stable usually do not indicate a major structural problem. Larger or expanding cracks could signal a structural flaw in the wall or a drainage problem that is undermining the foundation. Either way, if the problem goes unchecked, the result could be serious damage to your house. Look for new cracks or old ones that reopen after repairs, and monitor them (as shown above) to determine whether they are stable or active.

Finishing Rough Block Walls

1. Use a 2-lb. masonry hammer and cold chisel to chip off excess mortar protruding from seams.

2. Wash and rinse the block wall to get the best adhesion from a masonry-surfacer paint.

3. Use a trowel to fill joints with mortar where they have been left rough by the builder.

4. Use a stiff brush to apply a prime coat of masonry surfacer to patched areas and seams.

5. Use a roller fitted with a long-napped sleeve to work the surfacer into the rough-faced block.

Patching Small Holes

1. To make patch material bond securely to the block, chip away cracked edges using a cold chisel.

2. Brush away dirt and dust. Hold patching mortar against the wall, and then force it into the hole.

3. Smooth out small patches by running the side of a mason's trowel over the block face.

Filling Cracks and Holes

To patch a small crack, sweep out any loose debris and fill with cement. Fill any cracks that become wet with hydraulic cement or two-part epoxy filler. Hydraulic cement is easy to work with, can be used even on active leaks, and swells as it hardens to fill irregular voids.

A good procedure is to enlarge and undercut the crack using a hammer and a cold chisel. (Undercutting helps to hold the filler in place.) Then brush the crack clean and moisten it. Use a trowel to apply hydraulic cement or epoxy, smooth the surface, and then allow the filler to dry.

To fill a hole, shape a handful of hydraulic cement into a cone, squeeze the point into the hole, and hold it in place for several minutes until the cement hardens. Once you have made the repairs, you can refinish the patches (and the entire wall) with masonry surfacer or sealer. You should also fill openings around pipe penetrations. Caulk where the wall meets the floor.

Before adding the finished walls, be sure to seal openings and cracks in the foundation.

Repairing and Sealing Basement Block

1. To repair a leaking joint, start by chipping out any loose mortar and sweeping away debris. This will help the patch you apply grab onto the wall.

2. Fill a dry seam with fresh mortar, but use hydraulic cement to fill over an active leak.

3. Before the cement hardens, use a jointing tool (or any curved tool) to smooth out the seam.

4. Seal holes where pipes extend through the foundation by filling the broken-out area with cement. This also helps keep out unwanted pests.

5. Seal small cracks at the floor with an elastomeric joint sealant or a hydraulic cement patch.

Preparing Concrete Floors for Painting

1. Use a cold chisel and a masonry hammer to chip away rough edges of the crack.

2. Brush out dust and debris, which can decrease adhesion. You may want to dampen the crack or add a bonding agent before troweling in cement.

3. Use a trowel to fill the crack. Cement will do, although one variety, called hydraulic cement, swells slightly as it sets to make a tight bond.

4. Fill minor depressions in a concrete slab with flash-patch material.

5. Smooth out the patch area using a large trowel that can ride on the finished floor. You can feather flash-patch compound to a fine edge.

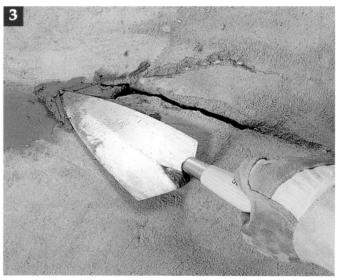

Painting a Concrete Floor

Paint is an excellent choice for those who want to keep remodeling costs way down or if the basement simply will be used as a workshop. A painted floor prevents stains from reaching the concrete itself, making them easier to clean. Paint also seals the surface against dusting, a powdery residue that sometimes forms on the surface of concrete. A properly prepared concrete surface, along with the right kind of paint, ensures success. Make sure the paint you use is designed for use on concrete floors.

Concrete gains most of its strength soon after being poured but continues to cure for years afterward. If the house is new, let the concrete cure for at least two years before painting it. Make sure moisture problems found in an older house are solved before you paint the floor.

Use an etching liquid to rough up a smooth, shiny surface. This product contains a mild acid, so follow the manufacturer's application and safety instructions to the letter. Rubber gloves and eye protection are mandatory. If the concrete already feels slightly rough to the touch,

Painting a Concrete Floor. Pour a modest amount of paint directly onto the floor, and spread it using a roller. Keep the leading edge of the painted area wet so that the roller strokes blend together.

use trisodium phosphate (TSP) or a phosphate-free cleaner to clean stains and heavily soiled areas. Then vacuum the floor to remove dust. Pour modest amounts of paint directly onto the floor; then use a medium-nap roller to spread the paint. The idea is to keep the leading edge of the painted area wet so the roller strokes blend together. Spread the paint evenly; otherwise, it won't dry properly. Apply a second coat of paint after the first is dry.

Painted concrete adds a finished appearance. Use paint formulated for this purpose.

Floor Overlays

If the surface of the slab has minor damage over a wide area or if the surface is too rough to serve as a finished floor, you can top it with a new surface. Overlay compound is a gypsum-based liquid product that's self-leveling (which is why it is sometimes called "self-leveling compound"). You pour it over the floor to a thickness of up to ½ inch or more, depending on the specific product you use, and spread it using a floor squeegee. The floor, when fully cured, is smooth and uniform. Follow instructions on the product label. Note that it's necessary to contain the product as it's being installed to keep it from flowing into drains.

Sump Pumps

There are two basic types of sump pumps: pedestal and submersible. A pedestal-type pump features a raised motor that does not come in contact with water. Instead, it sits on top of a plastic pipe that extends into the sump. Water rising in the sump causes the float to rise and turn on the pump. When the water level drops, so does the float, which then turns off the pump. With a submersible pump, the entire pump sits at the bottom of the sump pit and is submerged every time the sump fills up with water. A float on the pump triggers the on-off switch. Either kind of sump pump removes water effectively. Consult a plumber or supplier to determine the best sump pump for your situation.

Most wet basements can be fixed aboveground, without a sump pump, by improving the gutter system and sloping the ground away from the house. If your gutters overflow, clean them. If they leak, replace them. If downspouts empty near the foundation, install downspout extensions or splash blocks. If a raised flower terrace next to the house can't be properly drained, remove it. If a concrete patio slopes toward the house, replace it. And if the soil around the foundation does not slope away from the house for a distance of at least 4 feet (past the permanently absorbent backfill), haul in new soil and make sure that it does.

Once you've worked out a perimeter drainage strategy to direct water to the sump pump (either installing a perimeter drain in new construction or using a rented concrete saw and jackhammer to cut out 18 inches of concrete along the basement walls and dig in a trench, gravel, and tile in an existing house with drainage problems), you need to install the pump and attach the discharge piping.

Install the Pit Liner. You'll find two types of sump-pit liners on the market. One has perforations around its upper half; the other doesn't. Use the perforated liner for groundwater sumps and the non-perforated type for graywater pits. Dig a hole for the pit liner so that its top rim is flush with the top of the floor.

Cut an Opening in the Pit Liner. If your drainage piping installation was made on the outside of the footing, use a tile spade to tunnel under the footing, slide a length of pipe through the tunnel, and join it to the perimeter perforated pipe with a T-fitting. If it was made inside, direct the drainage pipe to the sump pump. Then cut an opening in the pit liner (usually at its midpoint), and run the drainage pipe through this hole several inches. Backfill the pit below the pipe connection with soil, tamping it in 4-inch lifts. Fill the upper half of the excavation with coarse gravel, packing as much as possible into the footing tunnel, if necessary. Finally, backfill the exterior, and pour concrete for the basement floor.

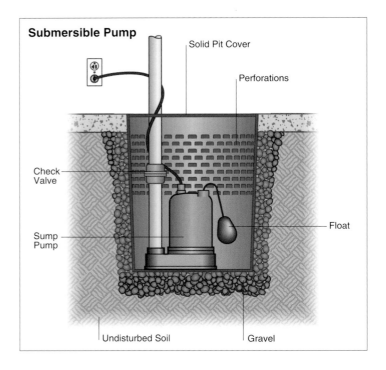

Pipe the Sump Pump. To install a submersible pump, begin by threading a 1½-inch plastic male adapter into the outlet fitting.

Set the Pump. Glue a 2- to 3-foot length of PVC pipe into the adapter to bring the riser up to check-valve level, preferably just above the liner lid. Lift the pump into the pit.

Install a Check Valve. If your check valve has threaded ports, make the connection with male adapters. If it has banded rubber connectors, tighten its lower end over the riser. Make sure the arrow on the side of the valve points up.

Offset the Riser. Before extending the riser, determine where you'll take it through the wall. The easiest spot is through the rim joist overhead. You may need to run to the right or left along the joist a bit to reach the best exit point outdoors. Offset the riser, and extend it to joist level.

Install a 90-degree elbow, and travel under the joists until you reach the target joist space. Use two more elbows to enter the joist space. Make sure this length of pipe has adequate slope.

Connect the Discharge Pipe. Join this pipe to the drain line with a coupling. Measure up the basement wall to determine the best exit point, and mark the rim joist several inches above the sill. Drill a ⅛-inch hole at the centerpoint to transfer the mark to the outside of the house. Drill a 1⅞-inch hole from outside, and slide a short length of 1½-inch pipe through the hole. Go back inside and secure the piping with hangers.

On the outside of the house, trim the horizontal pipe stub ½ inch away from the siding. Use 90-degree elbows to direct the flow onto a splash block.

Installing a Submersible Sump Pump

1. Cut a 3-in. hole in each side of the pit liner corresponding with drainage pipes, bury the liner, and connect the plastic perforated pipe.

2. Thread a 1½-in. PVC male adapter into the sump pump using pipe-thread sealing tape on the threads. Tighten the fitting until it's snug.

3. Cement a length of PVC pipe into the adapter, and lower the sump pump and pipe into the pit liner.

4. Install a check valve above the lid, and secure it with a nut driver.

5. Offset the riser pipe against the wall using 45-deg. elbows. This offset will help you position the pipe closer to the wall. Extend the offset pipe to joist level.

6. Run the discharge pipe outdoors through the rim joist, using couplings for connections. Cover the open exterior end with plastic screen.

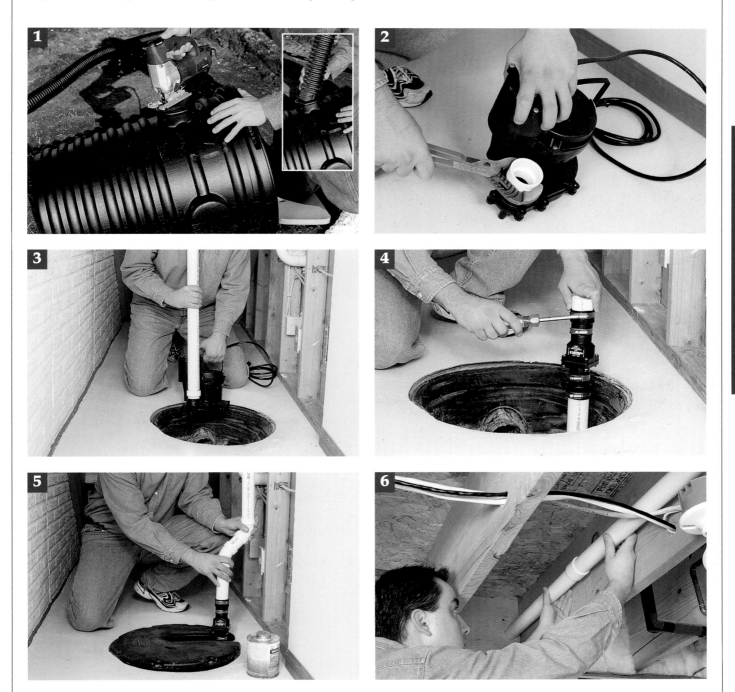

Basement Stairs

One advantage to adding new living space in a basement, rather than an attic, is that a stairway is already in place. It may be suitable just the way it is, but in some cases it may have to be rebuilt. In converting a basement, for example, you may decide to insulate the concrete floor with a system of wood sleepers and rigid insulation capped with plywood and carpeting. The thickness of this assembly will change the height of the last step on the stairs, making it shorter than the others by the thickness of the new floor system. Unless this problem is corrected, the stairs will not be safe and the project will not pass code inspection. In this situation, the stair carriage can't simply be raised, and the stairs will have to be rebuilt.

There may be other reasons to rebuild stairs. Although basement stairs in all newer houses have to adhere to the same codes as those anywhere else in the house, this was not always the case. If your house is an old one and the basement stairs are uncomfortably steep or poorly constructed, they must be rebuilt. Rebuilding can usually be done without enlarging the stairwell itself.

Basic Stair Dimensions

Your local building codes are the last word on stair dimensions, but the following can be used as a guide:

- The width of the stairs must be at least 36 inches, measured between finished walls.

- Nosing must not project more than 1¼ inch.

- Headroom must be at least 80 inches from the tip of the nosing to the nearest obstruction.

- For safety reasons, risers must be no more than 7¾ inches high and treads must be at least 10 inches deep, with a 1-inch nosing. In calculating the ideal ratio between riser height and tread depth, many professional stair builders use the following formula: two risers plus one tread equals 25 inches. Thus, a riser height of 7 inches and a tread depth of 11 inches would be perfect. Note that riser depth is measured from nosing to nosing, not from the nosing to the riser.

- Stairs with two or more risers must have a 34- to 38-inch-high handrail on at least one side. Handrails are measured vertically from the tip of the tread nosing. The end of the handrail must return to the wall or terminate in a newel post to mark the end of the stairs even in the dark. Balusters must be no more than 4 inches apart, preferably less.

- Landings must be the same width as the stairs and at least as long as they are wide.

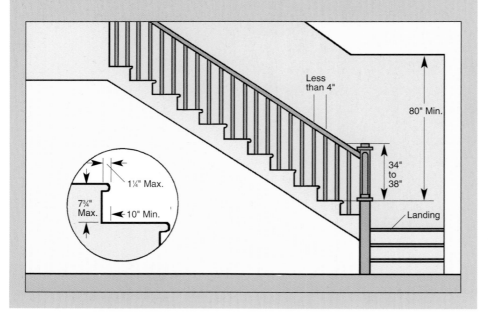

Adding a Balustrade

Many existing basement stairs may not be up to code. In particular, handrails and railings often are missing or inadequate. If the stairs are usable otherwise, however, balustrades can be easily added. Bolt the balusters directly to a stringer; then countersink the bolts or screws, and conceal them with wood plugs. Space the balusters so that the opening between them is no more than 4 inches measured horizontally. The top of the handrail must be easy to grasp.

Adding a Partial Wall

Another option is to enclose the stairs on one side with a partial wall that follows the stair pitch. A handrail can be placed on either the partial wall, the full wall, or both. Build the partial wall just as if it were a partition wall with a slanted top plate. Secure the stringer to the studs of the partition wall. Cover both sides of the new wall with drywall or paneling.

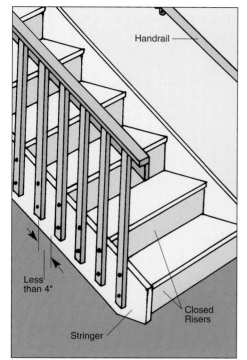

Adding a Balustrade. For an open balustrade, balusters must be fastened securely to the side of a stringer. Check local building codes to determine proper spacing between balusters; in most cases this is a maximum of 4 in.

Circular stairs are a good option when space is cramped, but check with the code authority before installing.

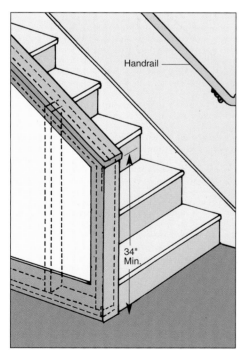

Adding a Partial Wall. A slanting partition wall can be used to conceal part of the stairs while retaining an open look. You must also install a handrail.

Stairs take up floor space, but open stairs such as these let you recapture valuable living area.

chapter 3
framing

Fastening Objects to Masonry

In the course of most basement remodeling projects, you'll be faced with fastening objects to a masonry surface. You might have to install shelf-support brackets or furring strips on concrete-block walls or anchor the bottom plate of a partition wall to a concrete floor. The task of fastening objects to masonry calls for special tools, fasteners, and techniques. The process may also call for a protective dust mask because it sometimes creates an abundance of fine, abrasive dust.

Hammer Drill. A power drill is indispensable when it comes to drilling into masonry. Consider buying or renting a hammer drill, preferably one equipped with variable speed, if you have to drill many holes. This tool creates a hammering motion as it spins the bit. The dual action helps shatter aggregate in the concrete and clear dust from the hole. Hammer drills often come with built-in depth gauges.

Drill Bits. You can recognize a bit designed for use in masonry by its enlarged carbide tip. Though more brittle than steel, carbide holds up well to the abrasive process of drilling into masonry. The flutes help to clear dust and debris away from the hole. Bits with "fast-spiral" flutes are the ones most commonly seen in hardware stores and home centers. The flutes are close together, but they're not suitable for drilling through wood and into masonry in one pass (as when setting wall plates). In this case, use a masonry bit with regular "twist" flutes. Some masonry bits

have reduced shanks that fit into standard ⅜-inch drills.

Not all masonry bits can be used in a hammer drill, however. The percussive action can damage or destroy some grades of carbide. Look for a note on the packaging to make sure the masonry bit you'll use in the hammer drill is approved specifically for this use. In other cases, some hammer drills will accept only a particular style of hammer-drill bit, referred to as "SDS" bits. These bits are designed to slide into the special chuck on some hammer drills. When the chuck is rotated to the locking position, the bit stays in place and is ready for drilling.

Star Drill. If you prefer to supply the power for your tools, or if power isn't available, use a star drill to punch holes in masonry surfaces. This tool looks like a heavy duty drill bit with a star-shaped point. They come in sizes ranging from ⅜ up to 1 inch. To use, hold the tip against the surface and strike with a hammer designed to use with the drill. Be sure to wear safety goggles.

Choosing Masonry Fasteners

At one time, the choice for securing anything to masonry was limited to lead anchors. These days, however, there are many products from which to choose. Nearly all of them fall into one of two broad categories: mechanical anchors that grip the masonry or chemical anchors that bond to it. For most fastening jobs encountered in the course of a basement-remodeling project, mechanical anchors work satisfactorily and are generally less expensive and more widely available than the more expensive chemical anchors.

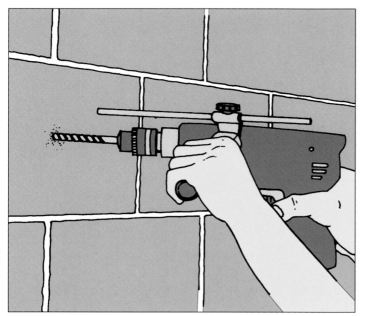

Hammer Drill. A variable-speed drill equipped with a masonry bit will bore holes in concrete. However, a hammer drill with a depth gauge will do the job faster and more effectively.

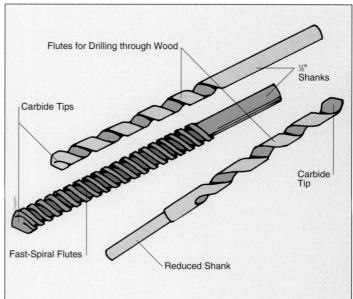

Flutes for Drilling through Wood

½" Shanks

Carbide Tips

Carbide Tip

Fast-Spiral Flutes

Reduced Shank

Drill Bits. The flutes show whether a bit can be used for wood (top) or only for masonry (middle). A reduced shank lets the bit fit standard ⅜-in. drills (bottom).

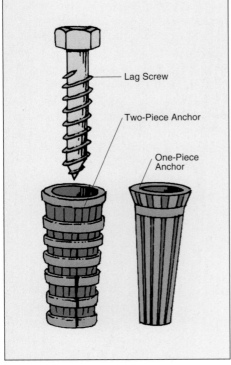

Lag Screw

Two-Piece Anchor

One-Piece Anchor

Lead Sleeve Anchors. Lead sleeves are available in one- and two-piece versions.

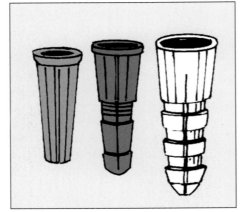

Plastic Sleeve Anchors. These are slightly tapered and hold better than lead sleeves.

Concrete Screws. Masonry screws have two sets of threads and a Phillips or hex head.

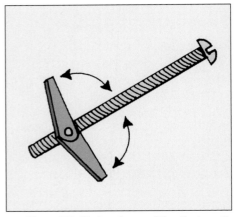

Hollow-Wall Anchors. The "wings" of the anchor fold flat so that the assembly can be inserted through a hole.

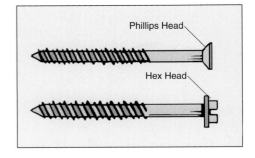

Phillips Head

Hex Head

Lead Sleeve Anchors. The kind of masonry anchor that most people know (and few love) is called a lead anchor. It consists of a lag screw and a lead sleeve, or shield, that fits into a hole that's drilled in the masonry. When you turn the bolt into the sleeve, the sleeve expands and grips the sides of the hole. These fasteners are readily available and inexpensive, but their holding power is limited. Another disadvantage is that two holes have to be drilled: a fairly large hole in the masonry for the anchor and a smaller one in the piece to be fastened for the lag screw. Use lead anchors to install shelf cleats or in other situations where the screws are not subjected to a lot of pulling force, particularly if only a handful of fasteners are needed.

Plastic Sleeve Anchors. A better anchor has a plastic sleeve instead of a lead sleeve. You must still drill two different-size holes, one in the masonry and one in the workpiece, but the hole you drill in the concrete for the plastic sleeve is usually smaller than the one required for a lead anchor, a distinction that makes a big difference if there are many anchors to install. A more important advantage, however, is that plastic anchors hold better than lead anchors. That holding power makes them a better choice for hanging heavy objects, such as cabinetry, from a masonry surface.

When using either plastic or lead anchors, the hole you drill must be just slightly deeper than the length of the an-

chor. If it's too shallow, the anchor can't seat properly as you install the screw or bolt and will not hold as well.

Hollow-Wall Anchors. When working with concrete block, it's usually best to drill right into the solid web of the block. This area offers the greatest holding power for sleeve-type fasteners. It may not be possible to guess where the web is located, however, or a fastener may be needed in a place where there's no web. In such cases it's best to use a hollow-wall anchor, sometimes called a toggle bolt. The most common version features a set of spring-loaded "wings" that are threaded to fit around a bolt. After the wings are slipped through a hole, they expand and grip the backside of the hole as you tighten the bolt. These fasteners are inexpensive but can be awkward to use. Once the wings are in the hole, the bolt can't be withdrawn without losing the wings inside the wall.

Concrete Screws. Though it seems implausible, certain types of specially hardened screws can be driven directly into concrete or concrete block without requiring a sleeve. These screws, often referred to by the brand name Tapcon, actually cut threads in the masonry. After drilling a pilot hole that is slightly smaller that the diameter of the shank of the screw you will be using, simply turn the screw into the hole as if it were a wood screw. Though they're relatively expensive and not universally

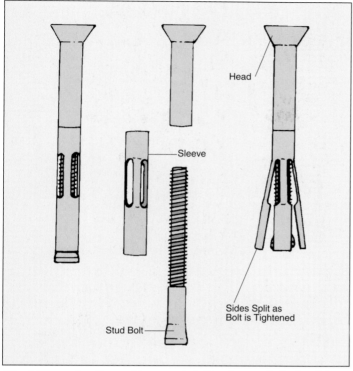

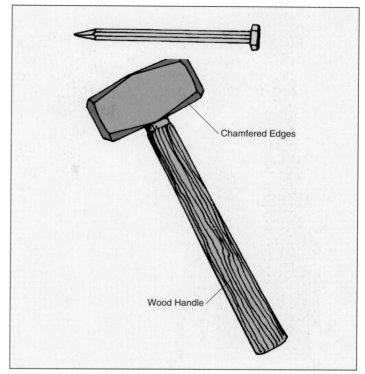

Stud-Type Anchors. You need drill only one hole for this kind of anchor. The sides of the sleeve are split, so when you tighten the bolt, they spread and grip the sides of the hole.

Masonry Nails. The nails are hardened to resist bending. The extra heft and special head of the hand-drilling hammer makes it the best for striking masonry nails.

available, concrete screws are well worth the effort it takes to obtain them. They hold as well as most sleeve-type anchors and don't require two separately sized holes for each application.

Stud-Type Anchors. Another kind of fastener that's designed for concrete installations consists of two parts. One part is a threaded bolt. The other part is shaped like a stud with split sides. You drill one hole through the piece to be fastened and into the concrete. Then tap the two-piece fastener into the hole with a hammer. After it's seated in the hole, you turn the bolt head with a screwdriver. As you tighten the bolt, the stud shaft expands and wedges itself in the hole. This is an excellent fastener for securing furring strips to concrete walls and plates to concrete floors. You need drill only one hole about ¼ to ½ inch in diameter, depending on the size of the fastener.

Masonry Nails. For speedy installation, masonry nails have long been a popular choice. These fasteners have a thicker shank and heavier head than standard nails of the same length; they also have flutes that lock into masonry. The holding power of masonry nails isn't great, but because it's so easy to install them, it's possible to use more of them. The nails are particularly useful when securing wood cleats to a wall and when fastening wall plates to a concrete floor. Masonry nails can also be used on concrete-block walls, but you should nail them into the mortar

joint rather than into the blocks themselves. Concrete blocks are brittle and tend to fracture and crumble when subjected to the stress caused by hammering home a group of masonry nails.

Because masonry nails are treated with heat in a special process called "hardening," they don't bend as you drive them into masonry. Hardening, however, means that you must never drive the nails with a standard framing hammer. The nails are likely to damage the hammer head, which can send razor-sharp metal shards into the air as you work. To avoid this situation, use a hand-drilling hammer instead.

Powder-Actuated Nailer. Perhaps the easiest way to attach wood to concrete is with a powder-actuated nailer, often called a "stud gun." These tools use a cartridge loaded with gunpowder to shoot a special nail or pin through wood and into concrete. Inexpensive hammer-activated stud guns are suitable for modest jobs, while buying or renting a heavy-duty model might make more sense for a big project. Newer models allow you to load a number of nails into the chamber. Many models allow you to adjust the power for different nail-driving jobs. The "gun" in the name should not be taken lightly. Stud guns are potentially dangerous tools if used incorrectly. Be sure to pay close attention and follow the manufacturer's instructions.

Installing an Insulated Subfloor

Most likely there's no insulation beneath your basement slab. One exception might be an unfinished daylight basement, where at least one wall is exposed to the grade. An uninsulated slab is uncomfortably cold in the winter, so contact the builder, if possible, to determine whether insulation exists.

An insulated subfloor installed over a concrete slab isolates the finished floor from the slab, resulting in a warmer floor and helping to prevent moisture from damaging the finished flooring. Using this method, strips of rigid foam insulation are fit between pressure-treated 2x4 sleepers that are fastened to the floor. Plywood is then attached to the sleepers. Either square-edge or tongue-and-groove plywood can be used, but tongue-and-groove plywood eliminates the need for blocking placed beneath unsupported plywood edges. Remember, there must be at least 90 inches of headroom (84 inches in kitchens, hallways, and bathrooms) after the insulated subfloor has been installed.

1 **Put Down a Vapor Barrier.** After sweeping the floor slab, cover it with sheets of 6-mil polyethylene plastic. This will keep moisture vapor from the slab from entering the living area. Overlap each seam by at least 6 inches.

Lift up the edges of the polyethylene, and use a caulking gun to put down dabs of construction adhesive to hold it in place.

2 **Install the Perimeter Sleepers.** Use 2¼-inch-long masonry nails or screws to fasten pressure-treated 2x4 sleepers around the perimeter of the room. If the lumber is dry and straight, a fastener or two installed every several feet will suffice. Mark these perimeter sleepers for additional sleepers 24 inches on center. This spacing is suitable for ¾-inch plywood.

3 **Install Interior Sleepers.** Align the interior sleepers square to the marks on the perimeter sleepers. Use one fastener at the end of each board and one about every 48 inches.

4 **Insert the Foam Panels.** Medium-density extruded polystyrene (EPS) foam is best for concrete floor slabs. Use a thickness that matches the thickness of the sleepers, about 1½ inches. Cut the pieces to fit between the sleepers, and insert them.

5 **Attach the Subfloor.** Use ¾-inch plywood subflooring. Cut the plywood to span across rather than parallel with the sleepers. Lay the panels in a staggered pattern.

1 Sweep the slab, and lay 6-mil plastic sheeting as a vapor barrier, overlapping the seams by 6 in.

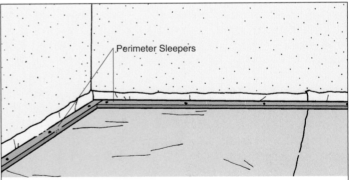

2 Nail 2x4 pressure-treated lumber around the perimeter of the room on top of the plastic vapor barrier.

3 Space pressure-treated 2x4 sleepers at intervals of 24 in. on center.

4 Cut 1½-in.-thick extruded-foam panels to fit between the sleepers, and lay them in place.

5 Attach ¾-in. plywood panels using 6d cement-coated box nails to secure the plywood.

Building an Elevated Subfloor

If head room is not a problem, you can build an elevated subfloor that consists of a plywood subfloor attached to floor joists that rest on the floor of the basement. For energy efficiency, fill the joist bays with fiberglass insulation.

1 Draw a Guide Line. Use a water level to mark a level point around the perimeter of the room. Measure up or down from one of the level marks to the desired height of the floor, minus the subfloor and finished floor dimensions. Cut a block of wood to this same dimension; use the block to mark off the floor height around the perimeter of the room. Connect the marks with a long spirit level.

2 Nail the Ledgers. Determine the size joists you'll use for the room. Lay a vapor barrier of 6-mil-thick plastic over the concrete floor. Overlap the seams by about 6 inches, and run the plastic up the walls to about the reference line. Staple the plastic to the studs; then nail ledgers, or rim joists and header joists, around the perimeter of the room aligned with the guide line. Use 16d common nails. If the span of the room is too great, build a girder by nailing together three layers of joist material with 10d nails.

3 Install the Joists. Nail joist hangers spaced 16 inches on center to the header joists and the girder if you use one; then set the joists into the hangers and secure them with 8d or 10d nails.

4 Insulate and Lay Subflooring. Install unfaced fiberglass insulation between the joists and flush with their tops. Nail or screw down ¾-inch plywood subflooring with the long edge perpendicular to the joists.

1 Mark studs at a level line around the perimeter of the garage using a water level (left). Measure down or up from the marks to the desired height of the new floor framing; cut a block to that dimension; and use the block to measure off lines on the walls (right).

2 Lay plastic on the slab as a vapor barrier. Determine the size joists you need; then nail rim joists and header joists of the same size around the perimeter of the garage, using the line marked in Step 1 as a guide (left). If the span is too great or you want to use smaller joists, make a girder from three joists to run mid-span (right).

3 Install joists 16 in. on center, using hangers on the headers and girder.

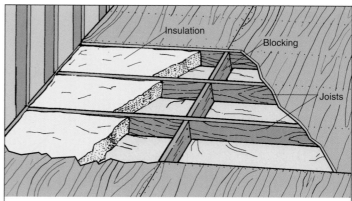

4 Insert unfaced fiberglass insulation between and even with the tops of the joists. Secure ¾-in. plywood panels perpendicular to the joists, using nails or screws.

3 Framing

Furring is an indispensable building material for any number of jobs. It's usually one of the cheapest things a lumberyard or home center sells, so it's the first choice for temporary fencing, holding roofing felt until the shingles are installed, and for straightening out walls that aren't flat, like the one shown here. This is often the case with basement walls that you want to cover with drywall or wood paneling. It takes a while to install the furring like this, but the flat walls are well worth the time. The hardest part is driving nails into a masonry wall.

1. Before nailing any furring in place, locate the high and low parts of the wall by pressing a 4-ft. level every 6 to 12 in. against the surface. If the level rocks, the wall is high, and you should make a straight mark. If there's a gap under the level, the wall is low, so mark this with a circle to easily differentiate it from the high areas.

2. Don't install furring over the high areas, but do run it over the low areas. Then add shims to fill the low area, using inexpensive cedar shimming shingles. Push the shingles together until the furring is flat. Check this using a level.

3. Fill the gaps with smaller pieces of furring to suit the material you are putting on the wall. The best nails to use are standard masonry nails because they are the easiest type to drive straight. But traditional cut nails penetrate the concrete faster, if you have experience driving them.

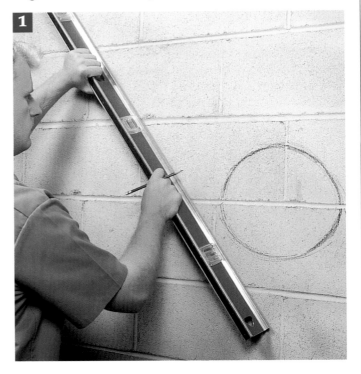

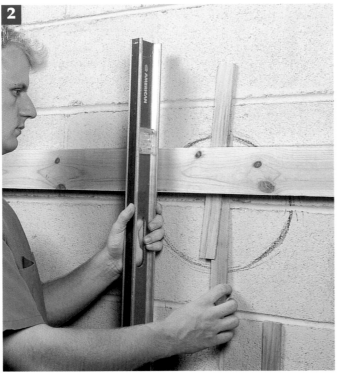

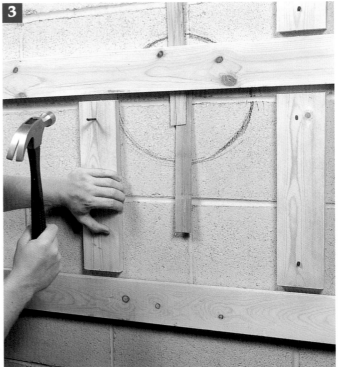

Insulating Masonry Walls

The basement—if it's built into a steep grade—is the coolest part of the house during summer but only moderately cool during the winter. The temperature doesn't vary much because basement walls and tall foundation walls are protected from temperature extremes by tons of earth. That coolness feels great on a hot summer day, but to be comfortable in cold weather, most basements require a supplementary heat source. Unless the foundation walls are insulated, much of that supplementary heat is wasted. All walls that face unheated space, such as the wall between a basement recreation room and an adjacent unheated workshop, must be insulated.

There are two basic ways to insulate the foundation walls: one uses fiberglass batt insulation and the other, foam panels. Most likely, it won't be necessary to install insulation higher in insulating value than R-11. Check with local building officials to determine the recommended amount of insulation.

When working with fiberglass insulation, protect yourself from the fibers that are inevitably released into the air. Wear a dust mask, eye protection, a long-sleeve shirt, a hat, gloves, and long pants during the installation and whenever insulation is cut or moved.

Insulating Crawl Spaces

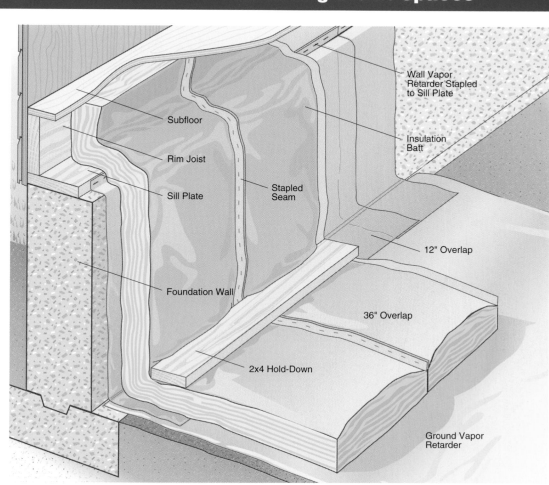

Subfloor

Rim Joist

Sill Plate

Foundation Wall

2x4 Hold-Down

Stapled Seam

Wall Vapor Retarder Stapled to Sill Plate

Insulation Batt

12" Overlap

36" Overlap

Ground Vapor Retarder

If your basement is adjacent to a crawl space, you will still insulate the inside of the room. But if the crawl space is also under a living area, which sometimes happens when an addition is attached to a house, you will need to insulate the foundation walls of the crawl space. If the floor above the crawl space is insulated, be sure to wrap pipes and ductwork in the crawl space in fiberglass insulation.

3 Framing

Insulating with Fiberglass

Perhaps the most practical and inexpensive way to insulate a foundation wall is to build a secondary 2x4 wall insulated with fiberglass batts between it and the living space. Use pressure-treated wood for the bottom plate. One advantage to building a secondary wall is that it's easy to run wiring and plumbing lines in it. You must take care in detailing the framing around windows and doors that are located in basement foundation walls. Before you build the secondary walls, make sure the foundation walls are free from moisture problems. Patch all cracks and use masonry waterproofer to seal the walls. Moisture that collects behind walls eventually leads to problems in the living area.

1 Check the Foundation. A secondary wall can rest directly against the foundation wall, but not all foundation walls are perfectly plumb and straight. To assess the situation, use a 48-inch spirit level to make sure the walls are plumb. Then with an assistant holding one end, stretch a string across the length of the wall and hold it about ¾ inch away from the wall at each end. If the wall touches the string, it's bowed inward; if the gap between string and wall is greater than ¾ inch, the wall is bowed outward. You'll have to make adjustments for this when you place the new wall in position.

2 Lay Out the Secondary Wall. You must position the secondary wall so that it's straight and plumb. Locate the innermost line; then measure 3½ inches into the room; and snap a chalk line to represent the face of the secondary wall.

3 Frame the Wall. You frame a secondary wall the same way a basement partition wall is framed, including the option of using 16- or 24-inch on-center spacing for the studs. (See page 50.) If there's a window in the foundation wall, adjust the layout so that there's one stud on either side of it. For the moment, leave out the framing between these two studs.

4 Shim the Top Plate. When you've assembled the wall, tip it into place, and align it with the layout marks on the floor. Use wood shingles to shim between the top plate of the new wall and the underside of each ceiling joist. Make sure the wall is plumb; then nail through the top plate and into the joists using two 16d nails at each joist location.

5 Nail the Bottom Plate. Check the position of the bottom plate against the layout lines and double-check the studs for plumb. Then secure the bottom plate to the floor using masonry nails, concrete anchors, or a powder-actuated nailer on a masonry floor or 10d nails on a wood subfloor.

6 Frame the Window. Cut a 2x4 sill to fit between the studs on either side of the window. Position the sill ½ inch below the window to allow room for drywall on the sill, and nail it through the studs on each side. If there's masonry above the window, you'll also need a header block set ½ inch above the window. Fill in cripple studs beneath the sill. To let more light into the basement, angle the drywall away from the window, so reposition the sill accordingly.

7 Install the Insulation. Apply pipe insulation to any pipes that run behind the wall, and install insulation in the stud cavities. The secondary walls must have a vapor barrier on the warm side of the wall. Use 6-mil polyethylene to prevent moist air from flowing through the walls and condensing on the cooler surface of the masonry walls.

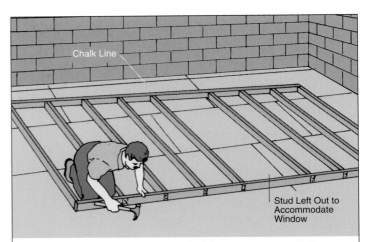

3 Frame the wall as you would a partition wall, but leave out studs as needed to accommodate existing windows.

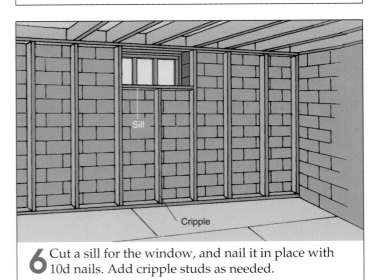

6 Cut a sill for the window, and nail it in place with 10d nails. Add cripple studs as needed.

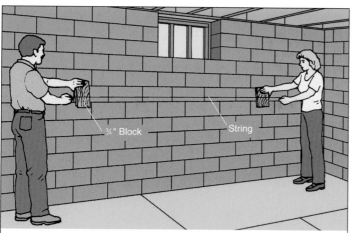

1 Stretch a string across each wall to make sure the wall is not bowed.

¾" Block

String

2 Snap a chalk line to mark the face of the stud wall. Position the line so that the wall stands clear of high spots.

Chalk Line

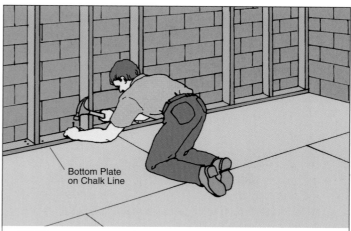

4 Tip the wall into position and drive shims between the top plate and the joists until they're snug to lock the wall in place (inset). Then nail through the plate and shims into the joists.

Chalk Line

5 Use masonry nails, screws, or anchors to secure the bottom plate in position according to your layout line.

Bottom Plate on Chalk Line

Insulation

6-Mil Plastic

Unfaced Insulation

7 Staple the flanges of foil- or kraft-faced fiberglass batts to the studs (left). Don't leave gaps. With unfaced insulation (right), staple 6-mil polyethylene over the face of the studs, overlapping the seams by at least 6 in.

3 Framing

Installing Rigid Insulation

Rigid insulation has R-values that range from R-4 to R-7 per inch and is made from a variety of plastic materials, including expanded polystyrene, extruded polystyrene, polyurethane, and polyisocyanurate. All of the products come in easy-to-handle sheets, and some are designed specifically for insulating foundation walls. Some products have rabbeted edges that can be held in place with 1x3 wood cleats. Although extruded polystyrene is highly resistant to moisture, the foundation walls must be dry before they can be insulated.

There are a number of ways to insulate a basement wall with rigid insulation, including attaching rigid insulation directly to the masonry walls; another way is described here and opposite.

The system features extruded polystyrene that's rabbeted on the edges and held in place with wood cleats. The insulation itself is 1½ inches thick and has an insulating value of R-7.5. The sheets are 2x8 feet, so you'll install the cleats on 24-inch centers. You'll also nail the drywall on 24-inch centers instead of the more typical 16-inch centers. Installing drywall this way works because it's fully supported by cleats and insulation. Check with local building code officials, however, to make sure this insulation method is permitted in your area.

1 Cut the Sheets. Measure for the cut, and mark it by scoring the insulation lightly with a utility knife. Use the knife to cut through the sheet. It won't cut all the way through, so break the piece off over the edge of a work surface. Cut 1x3 wood cleats to the same height as the insulation.

2 Place the Sheets. Start at one corner of the wall. Hold a sheet of insulation against the wall, and plumb it. Trim one edge, if necessary, to fit into an out-of-plumb corner. This first sheet determines how plumb adjacent sheets will be.

3 Install the Cleats. Hold a second sheet against the first, and slip a 1x3 wood cleat into the channel between them. Drill three or four pilot holes through the cleat into the foundation. Pull away the cleat, and deepen the holes in the foundation wall as needed. Clear debris from the holes, and use masonry screws to secure the cleat. Make sure the heads of the screws are flush with the surface of the cleats. Continue working along the wall in this fashion. Periodically check the insulation for plumb.

If you can't move small pipes or other obstructions, work around them by placing cleats on either side. You can fill odd-shaped spaces with expanding spray foam, but it must be a type that's compatible with the insulation.

1 Use a utility knife guided by a metal straightedge to cut rigid insulation. Support the insulation fully on a worktable; then snap it along the cut.

2 Start at one corner of the wall. Hold a panel against the wall, and plumb it. The panel must fit tightly in the corner.

3 Drill through the cleat into the foundation wall, and use concrete screws to secure the cleat.

Continue laying out the sheets, maintaining the 24-inch-on-center spacing for cleats.

4 **Seal the Edges.** Cut jamb extensions to a size equaling the combined thickness of the insulation and the drywall, and nail them to window and door jambs. Jamb extensions are slender pieces of wood that you nail to the jambs using finishing nails to extend them so that they are flush with the finished wall surface. Use a table saw to cut jamb extensions from ¾-inch-thick stock. Once you attach the extensions, use latex caulk to seal small gaps where the insulation meets window or door framing.

5 **Detail the Corners.** You must provide solid support for the edge of each drywall sheet, particularly at corners. At inside corners, place two cleats edge to edge with a square strip of wood in the corner between them. For outside corners, nailing strips must be the same thickness as the insulation—1½ inches—and at least 3 inches wide so that you have some bearing on the basement wall. Two-by-fours make good nailing strips in cases like these because they provide an adequate nailing surface. Secure the strips to the corner using screws. Code requires that all areas of rigid insulation that face a living space must be covered, usually by drywall. This is because rigid insulation is combustible.

Adding finished walls to a basement remodeling project opens up the design possibilities.

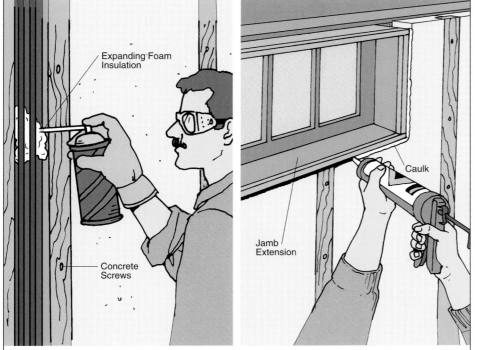

4 Use cleats to box-in plumbing pipes and other obstructions. Use expanding foam sealant to fill gaps. Wear gloves and eye protection; don't overfill gaps. Use finishing nails.

Expanding Foam Insulation

Concrete Screws

Jamb Extension

Caulk

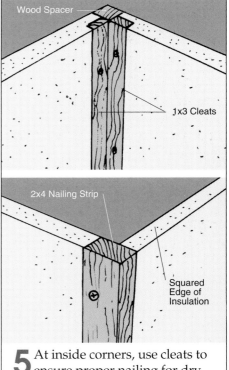

Wood Spacer

1x3 Cleats

2x4 Nailing Strip

Squared Edge of Insulation

5 At inside corners, use cleats to ensure proper nailing for drywall. At outside corners, nailing strips must be at least 3 in. wide.

Building Partition Walls

A partition wall extends to the ceiling, dividing the floor space. It does not, however, play a role in the structural integrity of the house. Usually, the walls in a basement are not large, so they can be built one at a time on the subfloor and tipped into place. Most partitions are built using 2x4 lumber with single top and bottom plates.

The Tip-Up Method

1 Mark the Wall Location. Locate the partition on the floor using a chalk line. If the wall will turn a corner, use a framing square to ensure square corners.

2 Mark the Stud Locations. Cut the plates to length. Measure 15¼ inches from the end of the plate for the location of the second stud, and draw a line with a combination square. Make an X just to the right of the line. The second stud measurement is shorter than the rest because the drywall will be pushed into the corner during installation. From that line, draw a line every 16 inches along the plates. To check your work, measure from the end of the wall exactly 48 inches. If done correctly, the mark will be centered on one of the studs.

3 Cut the Studs. Measure from floor to ceiling, and subtract the thickness of the plates and ¼ inch for tip-up room. Build the frame by driving a pair of 16d (3½-inch) nails through each plate into the studs.

4 Raise the Wall. Lift the partition into position by aligning the bottom with the layout lines, and shim the top plate where necessary. Nail 3½-inch masonry nails every 24 inches or so through the bottom plate into the floor. Make sure the wall is plumb. Nail up through the top plate and shim into the ceiling framing or into blocking.

1 Mark the location of the new wall on the floor. If possible, site the wall so that it runs perpendicular to floor and ceiling joists.

2 Cut the top and bottom plates to length. Measure 15¼ in. from the edge, and draw a line. Measure 16 in. from the line for each additional stud.

3 Cut the studs to length by measuring from the floor to the ceiling and subtracting 3¼ in. (that equals the thickness of the plates and ¼ in. tip-up room).

4 Tip the frame upright, and nail through the bottom plate into the subfloor. Check for plumb; shim where necessary; and nail through the top plate.

Forming Corners. To provide a nailing surface for the drywall, add an extra stud to each end of the wall that's part of an outside corner. One method of building the corner involves nailing spacers between two studs, then butting the end stud of the adjacent wall to this triple-width assembly. Another method is to use a stud to form the inside corner of the wall. Use whichever method you find most convenient.

Joining Intersecting Walls. You'll need additional studs to provide support for drywall where stud walls intersect. Add a single stud to the end of the intersecting wall and a pair of studs on the other wall.

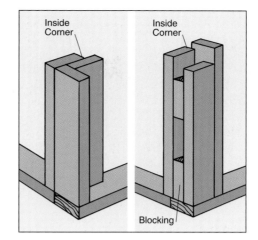

Forming Corners. Inside corners must have a nailing surface for installing drywall.

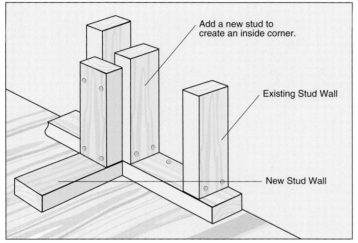

Add a new stud to create an inside corner.

Existing Stud Wall

New Stud Wall

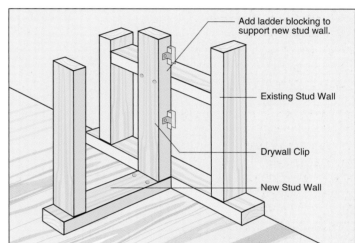

Add ladder blocking to support new stud wall.

Existing Stud Wall

Drywall Clip

New Stud Wall

Joining Intersecting Walls. Joining a new partition to an existing framed wall will require some work on the old wall. Open up the wall, and install additional studs as shown.

Other Options. Install a 2x6 nailer in the adjoining wall cavity, or nail up ladder blocking between existing studs as shown above.

Nailing Techniques

Face-nailing through the shoe or plate into a stud makes the strongest connection. It's also easier and faster than toenailing, where the angled nail sometimes can cause splits or miss most of the stud altogether. In fact, it does not make any sense to toenail unless the top and bottom plates are already in place. Either way, lay out stud locations on both the bottom and top plates at the same time. That way you will be sure that they line up properly.

Keep the frame from shifting by standing on the stud as you nail.

Start a toenail at a shallow angle, and steepen it once the point grabs.

Posts and Beams

All framing work must be completed before you can finish the walls. This preliminary work includes furring for concrete foundation walls, framing around heat ducts, and preparatory work around posts and beams that may be situated in the middle of a new basement conversion. Posts and beams are part of the structural system that holds up a building and must never be altered, moved, or eliminated without the guidance of a structural engineer. Those structural members are often in the way when it comes to remodeling plans.

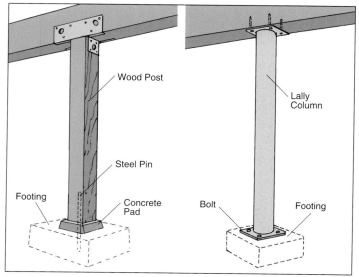

Posts. The posts located in a basement rest atop a footing of some type. A lally column is a steel post that ranges from 3 to 5½ in. in diameter. It's sometimes secured to a wood beam with nails that run upward through the top flange.

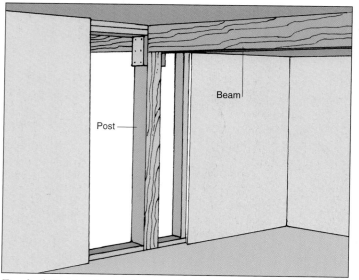

Buried Posts. A wood or steel post can be covered with partition walls. Unusually large posts might require a wall framed with 2x6 lumber.

Working with Posts

Posts typically provide intermediate support for beams. In most cases, they're found in garages and basements on top of concrete slabs that have been thickened to form a footing that distributes the structural loads. The top of each post is toenailed or bolted into place to prevent lateral movement. Posts in older houses are usually made of solid wood; those in newer houses are usually lally columns. A lally column is essentially a steel tube that can be adjusted to various heights. The columns range from 3 to 5½ inches in diameter and may be filled with concrete.

"Buried" Posts. If a post isn't ideally placed in relation to remodeling plans, try to revise the plans rather than remove the post. Moving a post is an option of last resort. One or more posts may be concealed by "burying" them in a wall that separates two rooms. If the post is unusually big in diameter, you can frame the wall with 2x6 lumber, rather than the more standard 2x4 lumber.

Concealed Posts. If it's not possible to bury the post, you can disguise it. You might nail plywood paneling or drywall to a wood post and treat the edges just as you would walls finished with the same materials. One possibility is to apply carpet to it using contact adhesive. Another option is to build a shelving unit around the post.

The post becomes a design element in this basement. Framing the post allows for the installation of thermostats and light switches.

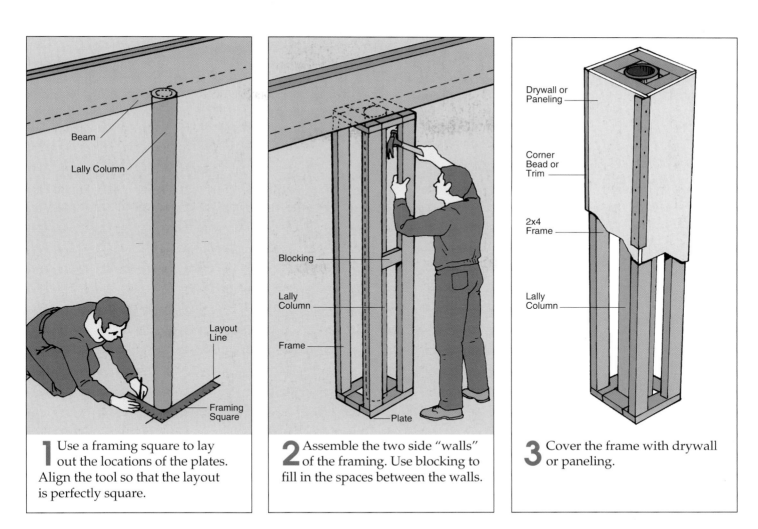

Beam

Lally Column

Layout Line

Framing Square

1 Use a framing square to lay out the locations of the plates. Align the tool so that the layout is perfectly square.

Blocking

Lally Column

Frame

Plate

2 Assemble the two side "walls" of the framing. Use blocking to fill in the spaces between the walls.

Drywall or Paneling

Corner Bead or Trim

2x4 Frame

Lally Column

3 Cover the frame with drywall or paneling.

Framing around a Post

One of the best ways to conceal a lally column is to frame around the column using two-by lumber. The frame provides a base for other finishes.

1 **Lay Out the Frame.** The outside dimensions of the box can be any size as long as the inside dimensions are large enough to accommodate the post. It's usually best to minimize the overall size of the box, however, to keep it from overpowering the room or taking up valuable floor space. Use a framing square to lay out the inside dimensions of the plates.

2 **Install the Frame.** Use 2x3s or 2x4s for the framing lumber. Assemble two opposite "walls" of the frame to fit between the beam and the floor. Using the layout lines as a position guide, tip the walls into place. Then use a level to make sure the frames are plumb. Nail the plates to the floor (with masonry nails or a powder-actuated nailer if the floor is concrete) and to the underside of the joists above. Cut blocks to fit between the frames at the top and bottom. Toenail the blocks to the plates. If the frame walls are at all bowed, you can add blocks halfway up the walls to straighten them.

3 **Apply the Finish Surface.** Once the framing is secure, apply drywall or wood paneling using nails or screws. With wood paneling, miter the corners or cover them with corner trim. Use standard corner bead when installing drywall to achieve neat, crisp edges. Cover the flanges of the bead with drywall joint compound, using the bead edge as a guide for your taping knife.

An alternative for posts: cover with plywood or solid wood and finish with moldings.

Boxing around a Post

Another way to conceal a lally column is to create a custom-made wood box to surround it. This method uses less space than the frame just described on page 53. It can only be used, however, if you've installed a plywood subfloor. The box can't be attached to a concrete floor. Use one-by stock to build the box; pine or a hardwood such as oak is appropriate. Base your choice on the final finish for the box. Pine can be painted or stained, while hardwood can be stained or left natural and coated with a clear varnish or sealer.

1 Lay Out the Box. Use a framing square to lay out the inside perimeter of the box. You can then draw the outside perimeter ¾ inch outside of the first line, providing the exact outside dimensions of the box.

Measure the distance between the floor and ceiling; then subtract ¼ inch from the measurement to provide a fitting allowance. If you measure the exact height between the floor and the beam, you won't be able to tip the box into position when you install it. Cut four pieces of stock to length. Use a table saw or circular saw to miter each edge at a 45-degree angle. Test-fit the assembly around the post.

2 Install the Box. Spread a thin film of wood glue on the edges, and use 6d finishing nails to nail three sides of the box together. Then slip the three sides over the post. When you are satisfied that the box fits, nail the fourth side into place. Toenail the box to the floor and to the beam above.

3 Finish the Post. Use sandpaper to round-over the edges of the box. A post is typically located in the middle of a room, and rounding the edges minimizes impact damage, both to the box and to those who may bump into it accidentally. It also makes a neater appearance. Use wood putty to fill all nailholes; then sand the putty smooth once it has time to cure. At this stage you can finish the post any way you wish. If you used a lesser grade of pine, seal all knots with primer and paint. Clear grades of wood can be painted, stained, or treated with a clear sealer.

1 Use a framing square to draw a full-scale layout on the floor. Use a table saw to miter the sides. For safety, use a blade guard (not shown here for clarity).

2 Glue and nail three sides of the cover together; then slip the assembly over the post, and nail on the fourth side. Toenail the box to the floor and to the beam.

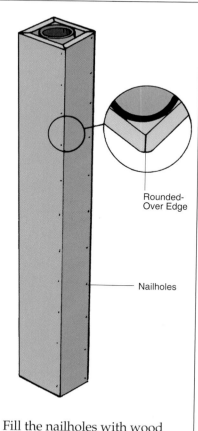

3 Fill the nailholes with wood putty; then use sandpaper to smooth them and to round-over the corners. Stain or paint the box to match the walls.

Concealing Beams, Ducts, and Pipes

The task of concealing a wood beam, like that of concealing a post, isn't difficult. A steel beam, on the other hand, isn't easy to conceal because it's difficult to fasten material to it. To get around this problem, you can secure paneling or drywall to wood framework that you nail to the underside of the ceiling joists.

Drywall on Steel. First build two wood "ladders" made of 1x3s. Place the ladders against the beam, and toenail them to the joists. Attach drywall on all three sides. Before finishing the walls, cover the drywall joints with trim or corner bead.

Wood on Steel. To make the job of covering the beam easier, use ⅜-inch or thicker paneling, ½-inch plywood, or ¾-inch solid wood. Attach cleats to the joists against both sides of the beam. Then use glue and finishing nails to attach cleats along one inside edge of the side panels, allowing for the thickness of the bottom panel. Nail through the panels into the cleats. Glue and nail the side panels to the upper cleats. Then glue and nail the bottom panel to the lower cleats.

Concealing Ducts

A large rectangular sheet-metal duct called a trunk often leads from a furnace to the farthest points of a house. Trunks are commonly found along attic floors and basement ceilings. Smaller ducts branch off the trunk and distribute warm air to each room served. The ducts in a central air-conditioning system may have a similar layout. If the ducts obstruct headroom, it may be possible to move them, but this definitely is a job for a heating-and-cooling contractor. In most cases, it's easier and less expensive to leave the ducts in place. With an informal decor, you can just paint the ductwork to match the ceiling color. It may also be possible to enclose them within the confines of a suspended ceiling. If not, you can box the ducts within wood framework covered with drywall or paneling.

Concealing Soil Pipes

The soil pipe, which is the main drainpipe of the plumbing system, conducts water and waste away from the house. Typically, it's the largest pipe in the house and may be plastic or cast iron. If possible, enclose the pipe within a box or soffit. It's a good idea to wrap the pipe in insulation before you box it in, especially if it's plastic. The insulation reduces the sound of rushing water. Be sure to take measurements in several places along the length of the soil pipe before making the box because the pipe slopes at least ¼ inch per foot for proper drainage. If the pipe's clean-out plug will be covered up by the concealment process, include a door for access to the plug.

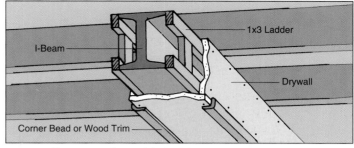

Drywall on Steel. Build "ladders" to support the drywall that you'll use to cover a steel I-beam.

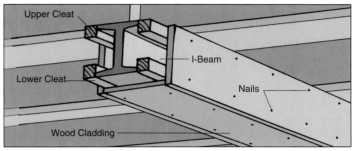

Wood on Steel. Use a simple cleat system to support solid-wood cladding around a steel I-beam.

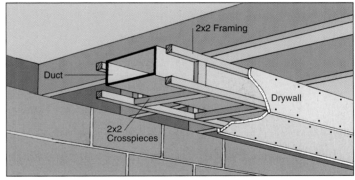

Concealing Ducts. Conceal heating and air-conditioning ducts as if they were beams. You can enclose ducts that run alongside beams in the same box.

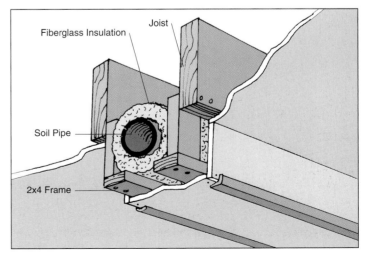

Concealing Soil Pipes. You can also box-in a soil pipe as if it were a beam or duct.

chapter 4

wiring & plumbing

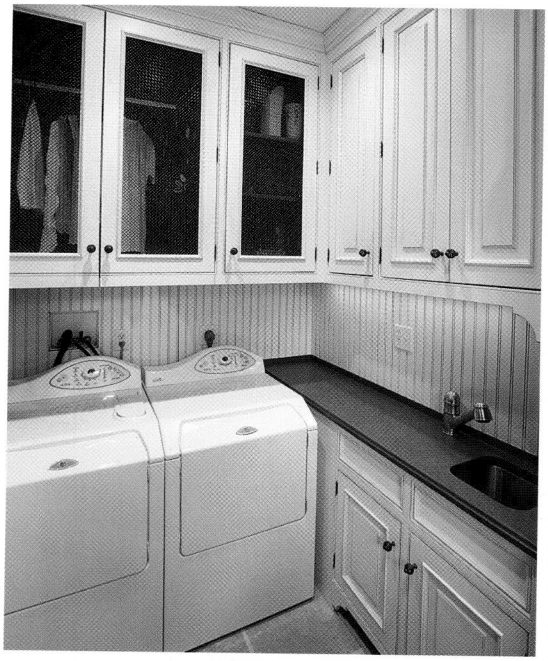

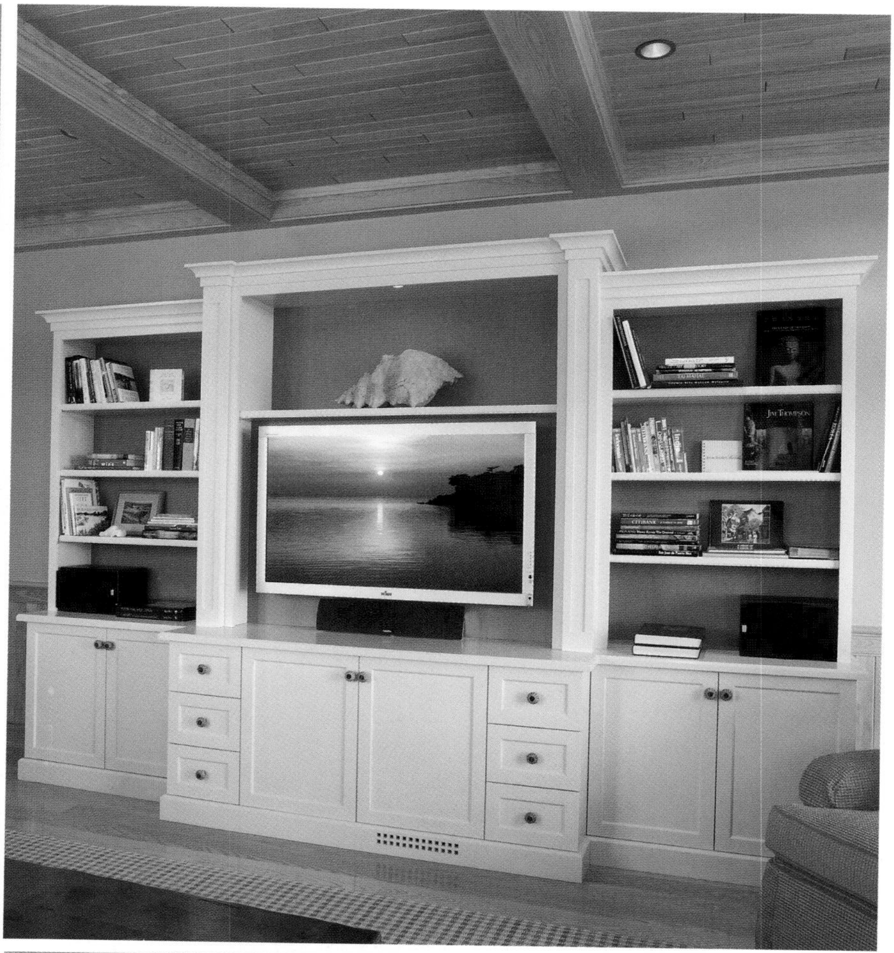

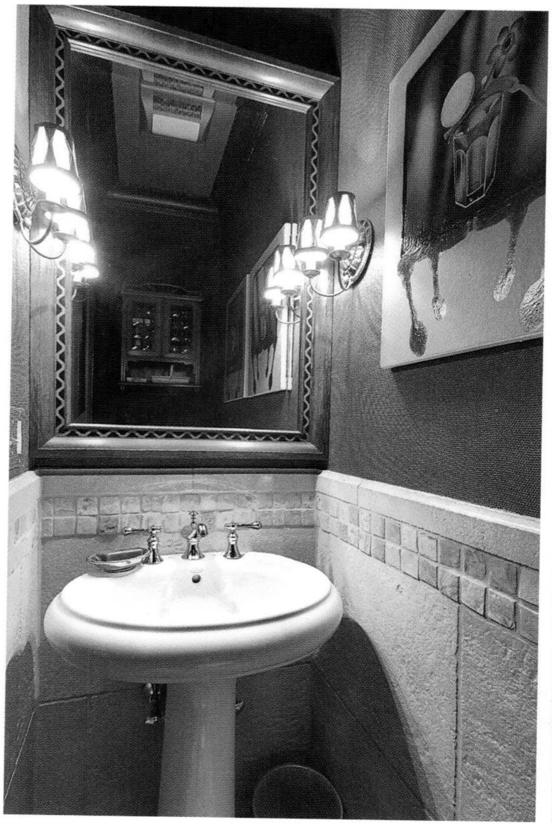

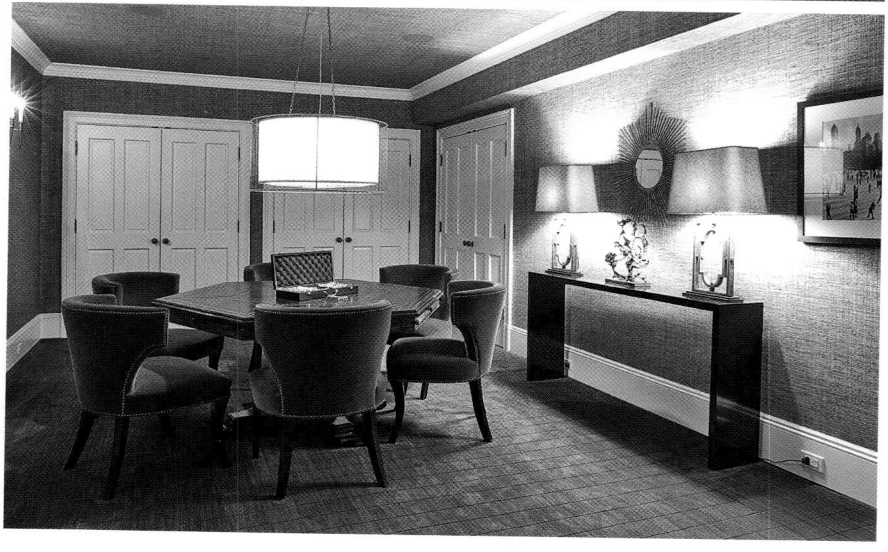

Wiring

Whatever the scope of your project, it has to be wired and lighted. In some cases, such as building a home office, the electrical requirements may be considerable. Once you understand some of the basic concepts, wiring isn't that difficult. It does require, however, that you pay stringent attention to safety and electrical codes. In some locales, only licensed electricians are allowed to work on household wiring, while in others a homeowner may do all the work on his or her own home as long as the finished project is reviewed and approved by an electrical or fire inspector. Be sure to check local codes before beginning work.

Additional Circuits. Although it's possible to extend a circuit to supply electricity to a finished basement conversion that will have modest needs, doing so may overload the circuit. Some codes, in fact, require that the renovated space be equipped with new circuits. Not only are new circuits safer, they also make the conversion far more convenient to use.

Service Entrance. Electricity enters the house through a meter that measures the amount of electricity used. It then enters the service entrance panel. The panel is essentially a distribution center that sends incoming electricity to various portions of the house. Each circuit is protected by a fuse or a circuit breaker that cuts power to a circuit in the event of an overload or circuit fault. Each circuit is inde-

Electrical Safety

- Always turn off the power at the main electrical service panel before beginning work.

- Always use tools that have insulated handles. Don't use screwdrivers that have metal shanks that extend completely through the handle. Even though the handle is insulated, the exposed shank can transmit an electrical shock to your hand.

- Never use a metal ladder when working with electricity. Use a wood or fiberglass ladder instead.

- Always use a voltage tester to test a wire for the presence of electricity before you work on it (even if you switched off the circuit).

pendent of the others, so when power is cut to one, the others remain unaffected and continue to do their jobs. To add one or more circuits you must route wire to the new living space, connect all the outlets and switches to the new circuit, cut power to the service panel, and add the circuit breakers. If you're not familiar with this work, consult a licensed electrician.

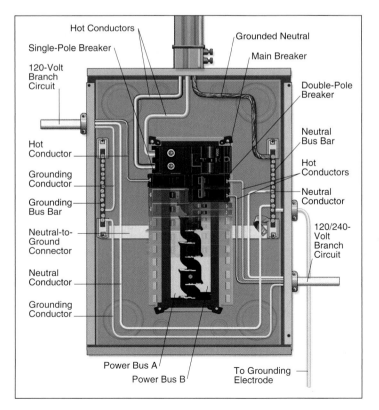

Hot Conductors
Single-Pole Breaker
120-Volt Branch Circuit
Grounded Neutral
Main Breaker
Double-Pole Breaker
Neutral Bus Bar
Hot Conductor
Hot Conductors
Grounding Conductor
Neutral Conductor
Grounding Bus Bar
120/240-Volt Branch Circuit
Neutral-to-Ground Connector
Neutral Conductor
Grounding Conductor
Power Bus A
Power Bus B
To Grounding Electrode

Nonmetallic Cable (NM)

Armored Cable (AC)

Also called the circuit-breaker panel, left, main service-entrance panel (SEP) is the distribution center for the electricity you use in your home. Incoming red and black hot wires connect to the main breaker and energize the other circuit breakers that are snapped into place. Hot (black or red) wires connected to the various circuit breakers carry electricity to appliances, fixtures, and receptacles throughout the house. White and bare-copper wires connect to the neutral and grounding bus bars, respectively. (Representative 120-volt and 120/240-volt circuits are shown.)

Pulling Fuses

A fuse puller is specially designed for the removal of cartridge-type fuses. The grips on one end of the puller enable you to remove cartridge fuses up to 60 amps in size, while those on the other end can pull fuses of greater capacity. You clamp the puller tightly around the center of a blown cartridge fuse, and then wrench the cylinder firmly out of its fuse box. The fuse puller is also used to insert the new or replacement fuse between the fuse box spring clips. This tool must be made of a nonconductive material, such as plastic, because the spring clips that hold the cartridge fuses are metal and can carry deadly current. Always be sure that the fuse box has been switched off before you pull a fuse, and take care never to touch the spring clips with steel pliers or any other metal tools.

To remove a cartridge fuse, grasp it firmly with a fuse puller, and pull it straight out.

Tools and Materials. Virtually all wiring jobs can be accomplished using a small assortment of basic tools. For running wire down to the basement out to the yard through finished walls, a fish tape is indispensable. You will also need a flat-bladed and a Phillips screwdriver, each with a nonconducting handle. Needle-nose pliers are perfect for snipping a wire to length and bending the end into a tight loop to go around terminal screws. Wire strippers are required for safely removing insulation from wires, and a voltage tester is essential for testing whether the electricity is on or not.

House circuits are generally wired with nonmetallic sheathed cable. The cable, which is flexible and easy to work with, is made of two or more copper wires wrapped in a protective plastic sheathing and sold in rolls of various lengths. Aluminum wire was used widely from World War II through the mid-1970s but is no longer considered suitable for household wiring. Consult an electrician before modifying an aluminum wire system in any way. Wiring is supported by heavy-duty cable staples that are driven into framing lumber with a hammer.

Before working on any circuit, test it to be sure that the power has been turned off. Test both receptacles on an outlet. It may be a split circuit.

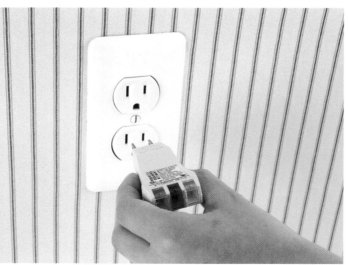

A plug-in receptacle analyzer checks grounded outlets for correct/ incorrect wiring. Three neon bulbs light up in various combinations to indicate correct wiring, open ground, open neutral, open/ hot, hot/ground reversed, or hot/ neutral reversed.

Choosing the Right Cable

The individual wires (called conductors) in a cable are available in a range of diameters. These diameters are expressed in gauge numbers; the higher the gauge number, the smaller the wire diameter. The more amperes a circuit is designed to carry, the larger the wire diameter requirement. Amperage is a measure of current flow. Circuits serving lighting and standard receptacles typically are 20 or 15 amps. Use 12-gauge wire for 20-amp circuits and 14-gauge wire for 15-amp circuits. Markings found on the plastic sheathing of cable explain what's inside and identify the kind of insulation covering.

Consider the following designation, for example: 14/2 WITH GROUND, TYPE NM, 600V (UL). The first number tells the size of the wire inside the cable (14 gauge). The second number tells you that there are two conductors in the cable. There's also an equipment grounding wire, as indicated. Each wire is wrapped in its own plastic insulating sheath, though the ground wire is most likely bare. In this case, the type designation indicates a cable that's for use only in dry locations; in other words, indoors. Following the type is a number that indicates the maximum voltage allowed through the cable.

Finally, the UL (Underwriters Laboratories) notation assures you that the cable has been certified as safe for the uses for which it was designated. For safety reasons, never use wiring or other electrical supplies that don't bear the UL listing.

Estimating Wiring Needs

Normally, service panels are relatively close to, or in, a basement or garage. Rather than try to calculate the length of this path, begin with a 50-foot roll of wiring, which in most cases is more than enough to reach from a panel to an attic or other area. The excess, if any, can be used for general needs once the basement, attic, or garage conversion is reached.

Stripping Cable and Wires

Wires are covered with insulation and bundled in cables. To make electrical connections you will need to strip away the protective covering.

1 Cut the Outer Sheathing. Place a cable ripper about 8 inches from the end of the cable, and pull toward the end of the cable.

2 Separate Wires. Expose the individual wires in the cable, and cut away the sheathing.

3 Remove Insulation. Use a multipurpose tool to strip the insulation from the ends of the wires.

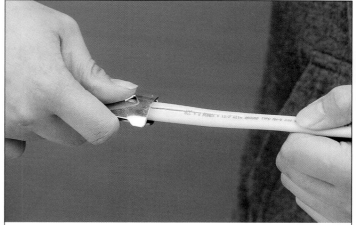

1 You can use a utility knife, but a cable ripper does a better job of removing the outer sheathing. Put the ripper in place and pull toward the end of the cable.

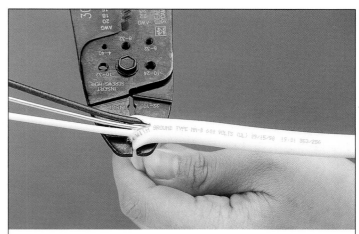

2 Pull the sheathing back to expose the individual wires. Cut away the sheathing with a utility knife or multipurpose tool. Don't nick the insulation.

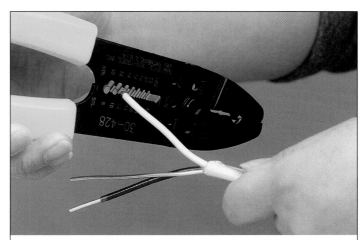

3 A multipurpose tool makes stripping the insulation from wires easy. The holes are sized for different wire gauges. Place the wire in the right hole, and pull.

Wire Connector	Color	Minimum		Maximum	
		Gauge	No. Wires	Gauge	No. Wires
	Orange	18	2	14	2
	Yellow	16	2	14	4
	Red	14	2	12	4
				10	3
	Green	Green wire connectors are used for grounding wires only.			

SMART TIP

Finishing a basement usually means adding light fixtures, receptacles, and changing the way the space is used. Before you let your plans get too far along, be sure to consider the location and the items placed around your panel box. The National Electrical Code requires easy access to the service panel to ensure that someone has an unobstructed path to the box in case of an emergency. Plan on an open space that extends at least 6 feet 6 inches high. There should be a clear area that extends 3 feet from the box outward. The box should be centered in an area that is 2 feet 6 inches wide. If moving the panel, do not install the new one in a bathroom.

Joining Wires

At one time, all wires in a household system were spliced together with solder and electrical tape. Now, splices are made by joining wires with plastic caps called wire connectors. The inner portion of each cap is threaded. Connectors come in many sizes; choosing the right one depends on the number of wires to be joined and the gauge of the wires. It's cost-effective to buy a box of wire connectors in the size most often needed rather than a few at a time. Have some plastic electrician's tape on hand. Electricians often wrap a turn or two of tape around the base of a wire connector to ensure its staying power.

1 Strip Away Insulation. Use a multipurpose tool to strip away about ½ inch of insulation from each wire.

2 Twist Wires Together. Using a pair of long-nose pliers, carefully twist the exposed ends of the wire together.

3 Add a Connector. Twist on the appropriate-size wire connector.

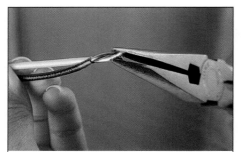

1 To join wires, strip ½ in. of insulation from the wires using a combination tool. Hold the wires parallel, and twist them together with pliers. Turn the pliers in a clockwise fashion.

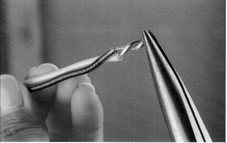

2 The twisted part should be long enough to engage the wire connector, and short enough to be covered completely by the wire connector when the wires are inserted into it.

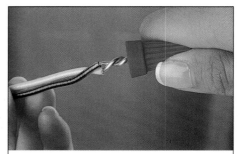

3 Screw the wire connector onto the wires until it feels tight and the exposed wires are covered completely. Use hand pressure only. Do not use pliers to tighten the connector.

Running Cable

Getting wire through the walls and floors of a house often calls for considerable ingenuity. Every house is different, but the following guide provides some techniques for solving typical problems. Running new cable usually requires notching or boring studs and joists. Check your local code before making any cuts, since the size and locations are often strictly limited.

Holes in Framing. Drill a ⅝- to ¾-inch-diameter hole in places where cable must pass through studs. If the hole is less than 1¼ inches from the edge of the stud, the National Electrical Code requires that the wiring be protected with a steel plate. When drilling through a joist, the hole must be at least 2 inches from the edge and not more than one-third the size of the joist width.

Cable Support. According to code, you must use cable staples to support the cable (generally at least every 54 inches on a run and within 12 inches of boxes). Be careful not to damage the outer casing of the wire as you drive the staples home.

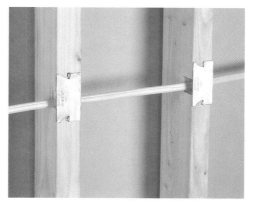

Holes in Framing. A nailing plate protects cable that passes close to the edge of a joist or stud. You pound in the barbs on the plate with a hammer.

Cable Support. Use heavy metal staples to hold cable in place without pinching it.

Wiring Around an Existing Doorway

If an existing doorway is in the path of your cable, you will have to run the cable up and around the door frame. In this situation, rather than cutting out sections of the drywall, you may be able to take advantage of the shim space. Remove the molding from around the door, gently prying it away from the wall. Use a rigid paint scraper with a scrap piece of wood under it to protect the wall. If you cannot remove the trim without causing it damage, you may have to replace the molding. If the molding is irreplaceable, you may wish to reconsider using this method to route the cable around your door. Once the shim space is exposed, notch out the shim spacers just enough to accommodate the cable. String the cable around the shim space; then cover the notched areas, using metal wire shields.

You can run cable around an existing door through cutouts in the drywall. An alternative is to take advantage of the shim space between the door frame and the jamb studs.

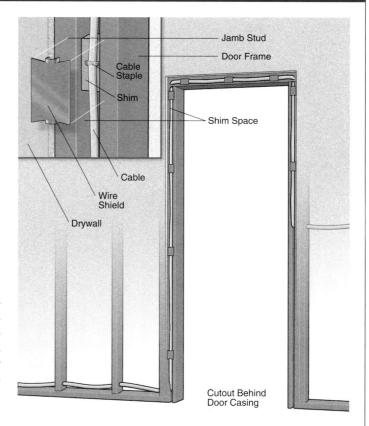

Jamb Stud
Door Frame
Cable Staple
Shim
Shim Space
Cable
Wire Shield
Drywall
Cutout Behind Door Casing

Running Cable in Open Walls

Adding floors, walls, and ceilings means the framing will be open so that you can run cable easily. You can also take the opportunity to replace outdated wiring. The easiest kind of wiring to install directly onto exposed framing is plastic-sheathed, nonmetallic cable, called NM cable or sometimes by the brand name Romex.

As a rule of thumb, you will probably get by with 14-gauge cable for bathroom lights and outlets. Special equipment such as whirlpools, heaters, and appliances will require 12-gauge wire or larger. Check with the local building inspector. Appliances such as these usually require their own dedicated circuits.

Before reworking any branch circuit, shut off the power to the circuit at the main panel or fuse box. Plastic boxes come with their own nails; use 6d nails for metal boxes. Mount them so that the face of the box will be even with the finished wall surface. Switch boxes are usually mounted 48 inches above the floor, while outlets are mounted 12 to 18 inches above the floor. In most cases, you'll need GFCI-protected receptacles. Check the local codes for any clearance requirements for the location of receptacles and switches.

1 **Plan the Run.** Drill holes for the cable through the studs; set them at least 1¼ inches back from the facing edge so that the cable won't be pierced by nails or screws. If you don't have a power drill that fits between the studs, you can cut out notches of the same depth.

2 **Install Stackers.** Run the branches to the fixture boxes by stapling the cable to the studs or by using cable stackers.

3 **Attach Cable to Boxes.** Leave 6 inches or so of cable ends poking out of each box to connect the devices later.

4 **Attach Clips.** Where cable runs up studs and just above or below each box, use a hammer to attach cable staples or clips to the studs.

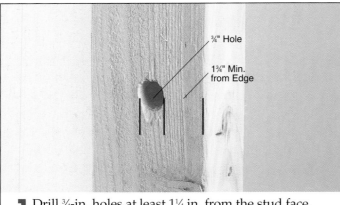

1 Drill ¾-in. holes at least 1¼ in. from the stud face. Special right-angle drills are available for drilling holes in tight spaces.

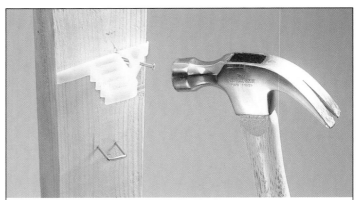

2 Attach plastic-sheathed cable to studs using metal cable staples or cable stackers. Stackers have channels that hold several cables.

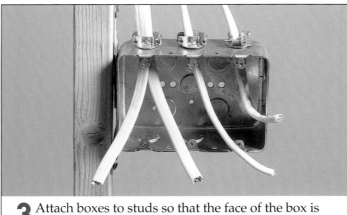

3 Attach boxes to studs so that the face of the box is in line with the proposed wall finish—½ in. or more proud of the stud.

4 Run cables through the framing in a straight line, if possible, and secure the cable to the framing with a staple every 48 in. and within 8 in. of a box.

Calculating Ampacity

An overloaded circuit is a real danger in any electrical system and can easily lead to a blown fuse or tripped circuit breaker. Worse, it poses a potential fire hazard and can be a threat to both your life and property. The NEC requires that the demand on a given circuit be kept below its safe capacity.

To calculate the total amperage of the circuit, add up those loads of which you know the amperage—it is usually listed on the appliance. For those loads that are listed in wattage instead of amperage, divide the wattage by the circuit voltage to get the amperage (amps = watts/volts), and add the values to the other amperage loads. Total amperage load for the circuit should not exceed the breaker or fuse rating. The safe capacity of a circuit equals only 80 percent of the maximum amp rating. For a typical 20-amp circuit, the circuit should carry just 16 amps.

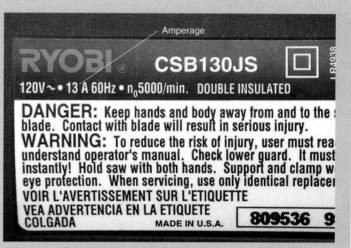

This product label provides information about the amperage used by the device.

Maximum Wires In a Box

Box Type and Size Electrical boxes must be of sufficient size to safely contain all enclosed wires. (Table 314.16(a), NEC)	Maximum Number of Wires Permitted						
	18 GA	16 GA	14 GA	12 GA	10 GA	8 GA	6 GA
4" x 1¼" Round or Octagonal	8	7	6	5	5	4	2
4" x 1½" Round or Octagonal	10	8	7	6	6	5	3
4" x 2⅛" Round or Octagonal	14	12	10	9	8	7	4
4" x 1¼" Square	12	10	9	8	7	6	3
4" x 1½" Square	14	12	10	9	8	7	4
4" x 2⅛" Square	20	17	15	13	12	10	6
3" x 2" x 2" Device Box	6	5	5	4	4	3	2
3" x 2" x 2½" Device Box	8	7	6	5	5	4	2
3" x 2" x 2¾" Device Box	9	8	7	6	5	4	2
3" x 2" x 3½" Device Box	12	10	9	8	7	6	3
4" x 2⅛" x 1½" Device Box	6	5	5	4	4	3	2
4" x 2⅛" x 1⅞" Device Box	8	7	6	5	5	4	2
4" x 2⅛" x 2⅛" Device Box	9	8	7	6	5	4	2
3¾" x 2" x 2½" Device Box	9	8	7	6	5	4	2
3¾" x 2" x 3½" Device Box	14	12	10	9	8	7	4

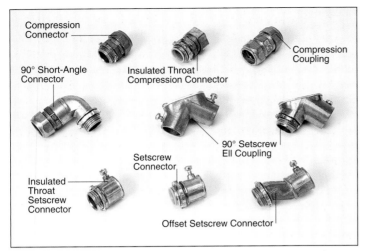

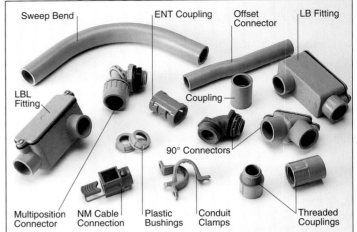

The connectors and fittings used to install electrical metallic tubing (EMT) are different from those used for rigid metallic and intermediate metallic conduit.

Some special connectors and fittings are required for rigid nonmetallic conduit and electrical nonmetallic tubing (ENT).

Surface Wiring

Building codes require that basements be supplied with a minimum of one circuit, though at least one additional circuit will make the basement far more convenient to use. A home office has considerable electrical requirements, so plan at least one circuit for this room alone.

It's difficult to run wiring and install boxes on masonry walls. It may be easier to build secondary walls against the foundation and run wire through them instead. If wiring directly onto the masonry walls makes sense, however, be sure to check local codes, particularly when it comes to grounding the metal parts of the system.

You can route wiring along the surface of a solid concrete or concrete block wall as long as it's contained in conduit or raceways that protect the wires from mechanical damage. Several types of conduit are available. Thin-wall electrical metallic tubing (EMT) is a particularly good choice for exposed wiring in a basement. Rigid nonmetallic conduit and electrical nonmetallic tubing (ENT) are other options, although you should check your local code to see if it is allowed for your particular situation. Raceways are modular surface-wiring systems that protect cable in enclosed plastic or metal casings. The modular ("kit") nature of these systems makes them more user-friendly for do-it-yourselfers, although you should check your local code before making a purchase.

Conduit Components. Each type of conduit requires the use of compatible components (including boxes, connectors, and fittings) that form a tight seal. The conduit is secured to masonry walls with straps.

Raceway Components. Raceway systems, which are more finished looking than conduit, use metal or plastic channels with snap-on covers to contain the wire, along with a series of fittings for changing direction and splicing lengths of track together. The only special tool you're likely to need is a hacksaw.

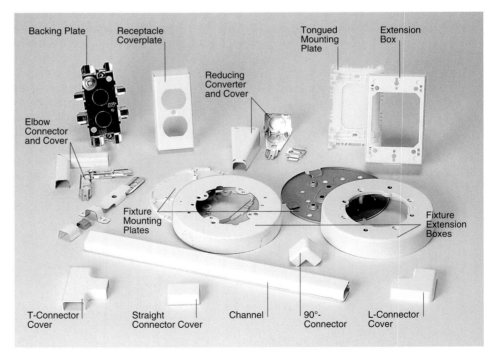

Typical raceway components include straight channel sections, elbows, T-connectors, extension boxes, plates, and covers.

Wiring Raceway Systems

1 Install the Power Feed. Raceway systems use single conductors rather than sheathed cable. You can use sheathed cable to connect the surface-mount system to the service panel, though.

2 Attach the Raceways. Begin at the starter box, and install sections of base track. Drill a hole through the base track every 18 inches and ½ inch from each end; then use it as a template for marking holes on the wall. Drill holes in the wall for masonry fasteners; then screw the base track to the wall.

3 Run the Wires. Tracks that intersect at an inside or outside corner are butted together. Turns on the same wall are mitered. Surface-mount systems use type THHN conductors instead of sheathed cable. Use clips to hold wires in place before you install the cover. The clips make it easier to install the cover.

4 Cap the Base Track. Cut lengths of base-track cover to fit over the base track, and snap them in place. Cut covers 1⅜ inches short of each intersection to accommodate joint caps.

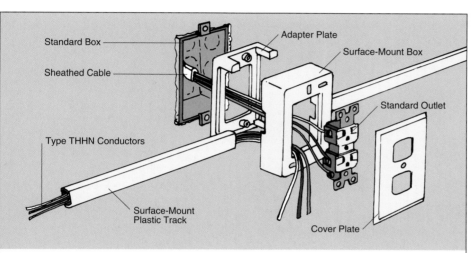

Standard Box — Adapter Plate — Surface-Mount Box

Sheathed Cable — Standard Outlet

Type THHN Conductors

Surface-Mount Plastic Track

Cover Plate

1 Attach an adapter plate to the existing box. Then install a surface-mount box, and connect the surface-mount track to it.

2 Screw the base channel to the wall with plastic anchors. At a tee, clip the edge to clear a path for wires.

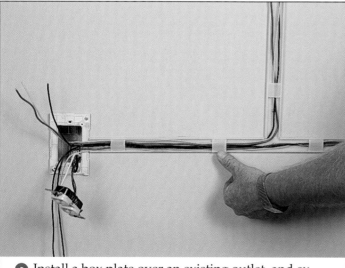

3 Install a box plate over an existing outlet, and extend wires from that circuit. Hold the wires with clips.

4 Once all wiring is in place, clip trim channel over the tracks. There are special connectors for T- and L-joints.

4 Wiring & Plumbing

Relocating Existing Wiring

In most cases, wiring already exists in the basement. In fact, most unfinished basements look like a hodge-podge of crisscrossing cables. These wires feed circuits elsewhere in the house and may have to be moved, depending on where they are and what's planned for the basement ceiling. This is one of the reasons it is important to commit your plans to paper before starting.

1 Remove Staples. Use nippers to grasp the edge of each cable staple; then lever out the staple. Avoid crushing or nicking the cable.

2 Notch the Joist. According to building codes, notches in the bottom of a joist must be no more than one-sixth the depth of the joist, and they must not be located in the middle third of a joist's length. Use a saber saw or handsaw to cut both sides of the notch just deep enough to hold the cable.

3 Place Cable. Knock out the waste wood easily by striking it with a hammer. If necessary, use a chisel to clean up the bottom of the notch. Move the wires into the notch. If necessary, use a cable staple to hold them. According to electrical codes, the wires must be protected by a steel plate that's at least 1/16 inch thick.

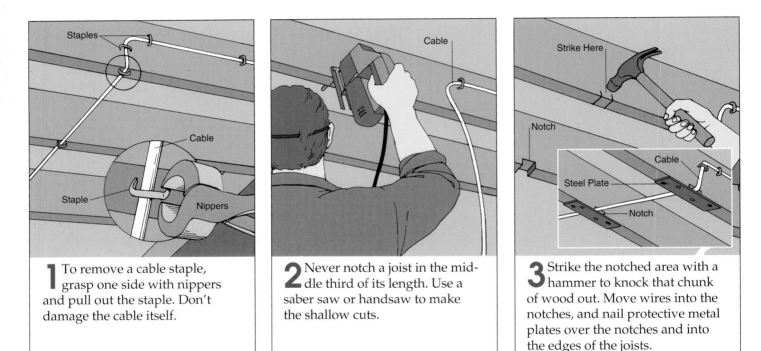

1 To remove a cable staple, grasp one side with nippers and pull out the staple. Don't damage the cable itself.

2 Never notch a joist in the middle third of its length. Use a saber saw or handsaw to make the shallow cuts.

3 Strike the notched area with a hammer to knock that chunk of wood out. Move wires into the notches, and nail protective metal plates over the notches and into the edges of the joists.

Preparing for Inspection

Once new framing walls are ready to be wired and electrical boxes have all been put in place, carefully begin pulling the cable through the framing. When you insert a cable end into an electrical box, leave a minimum of 6 inches of extra cable, cutting away the excess. Using a cable staple, secure the cable at a maximum of 8 inches above the single-device box. After you have run all cables through the framing and into the electrical boxes, rip back and remove the sheathing from the cable ends in each box; then strip the individual wires. Before a rough-in inspection can be done, you must also splice together the grounding wires using either green wire connectors or wire crimp-ing ferrules. Then place the wires securely in their boxes.

After a rough-in inspection is performed, install the receptacles and switches. Wait until the drywall is in place before doing this work. When the walls are completed and all of the boxes wired, you can install cover plates and turn on the power. Check each receptacle, using a plug-in receptacle analyzer, to verify that all of the wiring has been properly done. Install the light fixtures; then confirm that they are all working. Once you have completed all of this, your work will be ready for final inspection. The inspector will reexamine your work, performing many of the same circuit tests as you.

Incoming (LINE) Hot Wire

Incoming (LINE) Neutral Wire

Outgoing (LOAD) Neutral Wire

Outgoing (LOAD) Hot Wire

Ground-Fault Circuit Interrupters (GFCI). Although a powerful current surging through a grounding system will melt (blow) a fuse or switch off (trip) a circuit breaker, a less powerful current may not be sufficient to do this. The risk of this happening is especially great in moisture-prone locations. To protect against this danger, use what is called a ground-fault circuit interrupter, or GFCI, left. If the amperage flowing through the black and white wires is equal, then the circuit is operating properly. But if the GFCI detects as little as a 0.005-amp difference between the two wires, then the device breaks the circuit almost instantly. Incoming hot and neutral wires are connected to their respective terminals marked LINE. Outgoing wires, if any, are connected to the LOAD terminals.

Installing Receptacles

New receptacles accepted by the National Electrical Code contain three slots: two vertical slots of slightly different length for the hot and neutral wires, and a U-shaped slot for the ground wire. You'll need special ground-fault circuit-interrupter (GFCI) receptacles for basement areas, bathrooms, and other areas near water or below ground. Like a supersensitive circuit breaker, a GFCI cuts current in a fraction of a second if a short occurs.

Wiring Middle-of-Run Receptacles

The conventional way to wire a middle-of-run receptacle is to connect all of the wires to the receptacle, letting it act as the splice between the connecting black or white wires. Wiring a receptacle this way is easy but connects all of the devices on the circuit in a series—if you temporarily remove one receptacle or it should malfunction, the current to the rest of the line will be cut. Alternatively, wire the receptacles on the circuit independently. Splice each pair of hot and neutral wires using wire connectors; then connect a pigtail from each splice to the appropriate receptacle terminal. If you remove the receptacle from the circuit, the rest of the circuit will continue to work.

Pull the Cable Ends, and Strip the Cable and Wires. Bring the ends of the two cables into the box. Secure the cables with cable clamps if the box isn't self-clamping. Rip the sheathing back on the cable, and strip the inside wires.

Wire and Ground the Receptacle. Connect the two black hot wires to the brass screw terminals and the two

white neutral wires to the silver screw terminals. Using a green wire connector, splice together the cable grounding wires and two pigtail grounding wires—one from the receptacle, and another from the grounding screw (if you are using a metal box).

End-of-Run Receptacles

Bring the end of the wire cable into the box. Secure the cable, using cable clamps. Rip the sheathing back on the cable, and strip the inside wires.

Wire and Ground the Receptacle. Connect the black hot wire to a brass screw terminal and the white neutral wire to a silver screw terminal. Splice together the cable grounding wire and two pigtail grounding wires—one from the receptacle, and another from the grounding screw (if you are using a metal box).

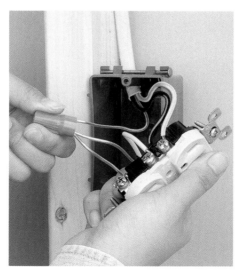

Wiring Middle-of-Run Receptacles. Connect the two black wires to the two brass-colored screws and the two white wires to the two silver-colored terminals.

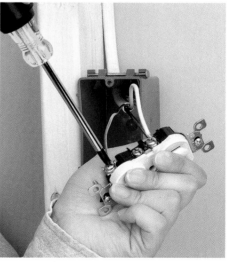

Wiring End-of-Run Receptacles. Bring the incoming cable into the box. Connect the black wire to a brass-colored screw and the white wire to a silver-colored screw.

Wiring Fixtures

Wiring lighting fixtures or any electrical appliance in a permanent location requires bringing a power supply cable to the fixture, wiring in a switch, and attaching the fixture to the wall or ceiling. You can wire a remote switch by running the power cable through the switch and into the fixture (in-line wiring) or by running the power cable to the fixture first, then taking a "leg" off the hot wire to the switch.

Wiring a Fixture in Line

1 **Bring a Cable to the Switch.** Bring a power cable from a junction box or receptacle into the switch box. Run an outgoing cable from the switch box into the fixture box. Connect the hot (black) wire from the power cable to the side of the switch marked "hot" or "black." Connect the black wire of the outgoing cable to the other hot terminal. Splice the two neutral (white) wires using a plastic wire connector. Splice the grounding (bare) wires using a plastic wire connector, and attach a short length to the green grounding screw inside the box (if metal).

2 **Connect the Cable to the Fixture.** Bring the cable from the switch into the fixture box, and attach the black and white cable wires to fixture wires of the same color using plastic wire connectors. Connect the ground wire to the box (if metal). In plastic boxes, connect the ground wire from the fixture to the ground wire of the cable, if the fixture has a ground wire.

Two common methods for attaching incandescent ceiling and wall lamps are shown. Begin by screwing a cross strap across the box. If the fixture base has screws at the sides, position the base so that these screws align with the two holes in the cross strap. If the lamp has a nipple in the center, screw the nipple into the center hole in the cross strap of the box. Then place the base and lens over the nipple.

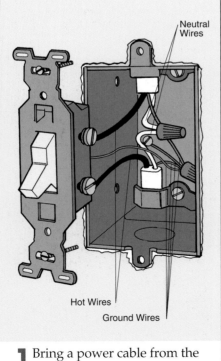

1 Bring a power cable from the power source (junction box or receptacle) into the switch box. Then run an outgoing cable from the switch box to the fixture box.

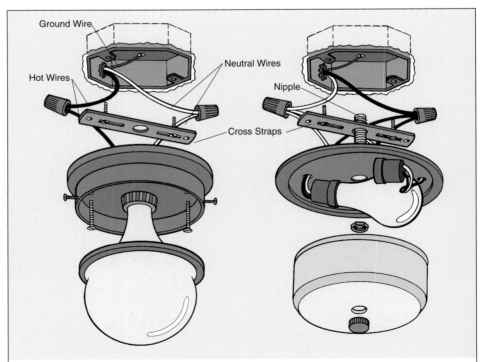

2 Bring the cable from the switch into the fixture box, and connect the wires. Attach incandescent ceiling and wall lamps to the cross strap with screws (left) or to a nipple screwed into the strap (right).

Wiring a Fixture Switched from a Loop

Sometimes you must run the power cable directly to the fixture and run a loop cable from the fixture to the switch.

1 **Run the Cables.** Bring a power cable into the fixture box, and strip the wire ends. Run a separate loop cable from the fixture box into the switch box, and strip the wire ends.

2 **Connect the Power Cable.** Connect the white wire from the power cable to the white lead of the fixture. Connect the black fixture wire to the black wire of the switch-loop cable. Then connect the white wire from the switch loop to the black power lead. Mark the end of this wire as "black" by wrapping it with electrical tape. Finally, connect the ground wire from the power cable to the ground wire of the switch loop and to the grounding screw on the box (if metal).

3 **Connect the Switch.** Connect the black and white wires from the switch-loop cable to the switch. Code the white wire as "black" by wrapping the end with electrical tape. Connect the ground wire to the grounding screw in the box (if metal).

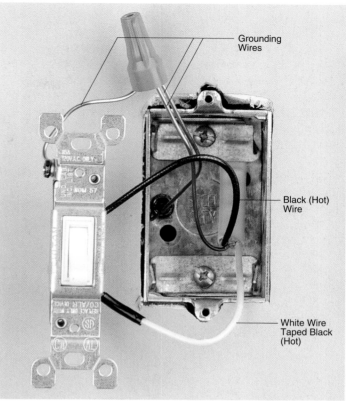

Grounding Wires

Black (Hot) Wire

White Wire Taped Black (Hot)

At the end of a circuit, both the black and white wires connecting to a switch are hot. To indicate this, wrap the white wire with black tape.

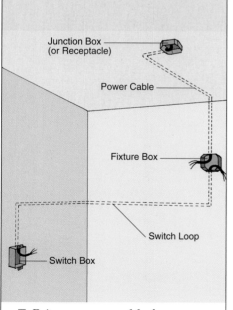

Junction Box (or Receptacle)

Power Cable

Fixture Box

Switch Loop

Switch Box

1 Bring a power cable from a source, such as a receptacle or junction box, into the fixture box; then run a switch-loop cable from the fixture box to the switch box.

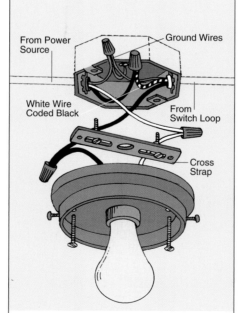

From Power Source

Ground Wires

White Wire Coded Black

From Switch Loop

Cross Strap

2 To wire a lamp controlled by a switch loop, connect the white power wire to the white fixture wire and the black power wire to the marked white loop wire.

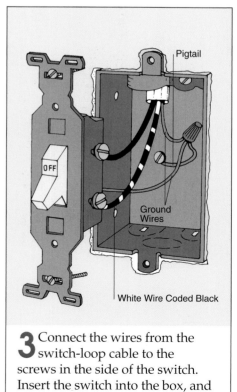

Pigtail

OFF

Ground Wires

White Wire Coded Black

3 Connect the wires from the switch-loop cable to the screws in the side of the switch. Insert the switch into the box, and tighten the screws.

Plumbing

As with wiring, plumbing pipes must be installed before walls, ceilings, or floors are covered. A household plumbing system consists of a hot and cold water supply furnished through tubing by way of a well or municipal water system, and a vent and drainage network designed to carry waste away from the house to a municipal sewer or private septic system. Although related, each system is independent. Pumps force fresh water through tubing under controlled pressure, so the tubing can be installed at any angle and in any direction. Waste is carried to septic systems or sewers through gravity flow, so waste pipes must run downhill from fixtures to main sewer or septic lines at a slope of 1/8 to 1/4 inch per foot, depending on the size of the pipe.

Waste pipes (commonly referred to as the drain-waste-vent, or DWV, system) must be vented to the atmosphere so air pressure within the network of DWV pipes is equalized. Vents prevent airlocks so water can drain freely and prevent water in plumbing traps from being siphoned out. Every plumbing fixture in a house has a trap that should stay filled with water to block the passage of sewer or septic-tank gases into the house.

Basement Bathrooms. For those experienced in cutting and soldering pipe, the job of adding tubing to supply water to a basement lavatory or toilet is straightforward. Providing a drain and vent for the waste water, however, remains a difficult job. Getting waste to a main sewer or septic line above the basement floor may require the installation of a pump system.

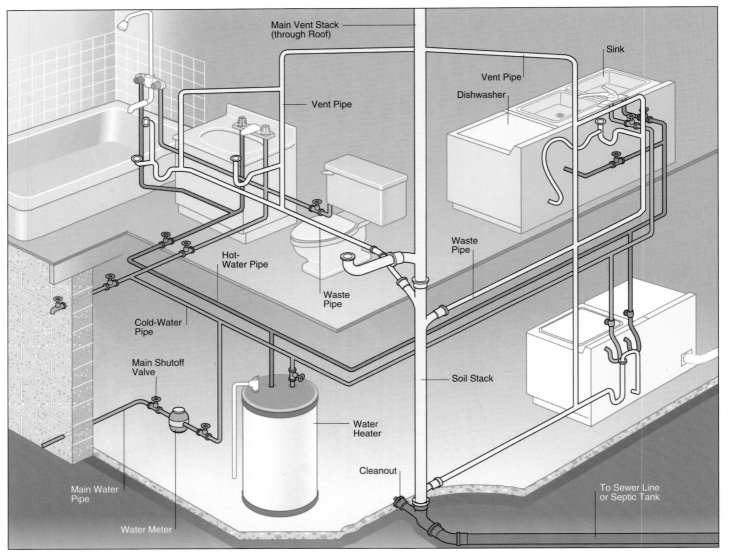

Here is a typical household plumbing system. Water arrives from the municipal system or a private well. The cold-water supply lines branch from this main line; hot-water lines are first routed through the water heater. All fixtures receiving water are also connected to drainpipes and vent pipes. All drain and vent lines converge on the soil stack, which extends through the roof.

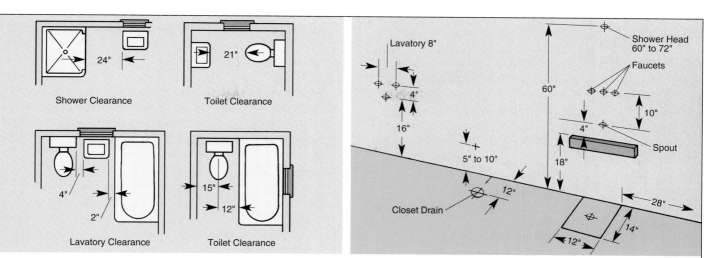

1 In making the layout, be sure to allow ample clearance between fixtures. Shown are the minimum clearances recommended between bathroom fixtures. When roughing-in plumbing for a new bathroom, first establish the location of each fixture, noting the positions of drains and faucets so stub-outs can be cut through walls and floors at the exact spots they are needed.

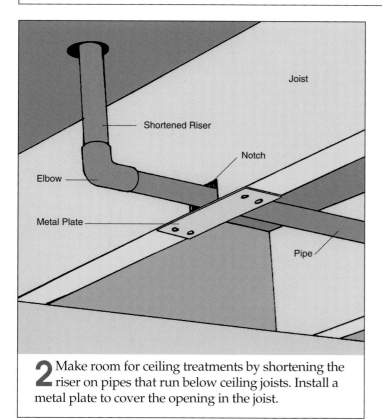

2 Make room for ceiling treatments by shortening the riser on pipes that run below ceiling joists. Install a metal plate to cover the opening in the joist.

Getting Started

During the planning stage for your new bathroom, draw up a detailed plan to scale. Once the plan has been prepared, along with a list of parts and materials, have someone with experience in doing a similar project check to see whether anything has been overlooked. The plumbing supply store with which you do business may have trained consultants on staff who can provide such a service.

1 **Put Your Plans on Paper.** After deciding where new fixtures and appliances are to go, make plan-view and elevation drawings. In planning the layout, leave ample clearance between fixtures. Elevations should include placement of all plumbing fixtures. Get a copy of your local plumbing code from the building department. You'll find information regarding sizing and slope of pipes, venting methods, cleanout plug placement, and the like.

Make notes on your plan of the type of water delivery and DWV pipes already in your home. Consult your local code to determine whether new pipes and fittings have to be the same type as the existing ones, or whether it's permissible to switch to a different type with which it will be easier to work. Specifically, does the code permit the integration of plastic DWV pipe with an existing cast-iron drain system? Plan to use copper tubing for all water-delivery piping.

2 **Move Pipes.** In most basements, water pipes run along the underside of the ceiling joist. To move them up so that you can attach drywall to the underside of the joists, shorten the riser of the pipe that extends up into the floor above. Then notch the joists in the pipe run. Solder a new elbow to the riser and the horizontal pipe. Attach a metal plate to the joist for protection.

Running Copper
Water Supply Tubing

The hot and cold water supplied to fixtures throughout the house runs through copper tubing (sometimes galvanized-steel pipe in older houses, in which case you should replace the piping). After tapping into an existing line, simply solder lengths of copper tubing together until the fixture is reached.

Cutting Copper Pipe

1 Cut the Tubing. You can cut copper pipe using a tubing cutter or hacksaw. To use a tubing cutter, gradually tighten the cutting blade against the pipe as you rotate the tool several times until the pipe snaps apart. To use a hacksaw, place the pipe on a grooved board or in a miter box to make a straight cut and prevent the pipe from rolling.

2 Remove the Burrs. After cutting, you need to remove the burrs from inside the pipe. Some tubing cutters contain a burr remover.

3 Clean the Pipe before Soldering. Use a wire brush to clean the insides of the pipe and the fitting to which the pipe will be joined. Before soldering, clean the ends of the pipe with emery cloth or a multipurpose plumber's tool, which contains an abrasive ring for cleaning the outside of the pipe and a brush for the inside.

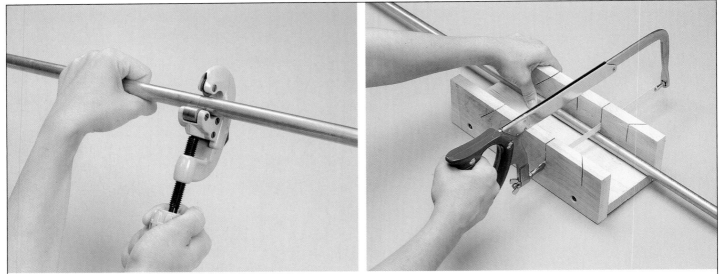

1 To cut a copper pipe with a tubing cutter, gradually tighten the cutting blade against the pipe, and rotate the tool several times. If you cut a copper pipe with a hacksaw, remember to place the pipe on a grooved board or in a miter box for easier cutting.

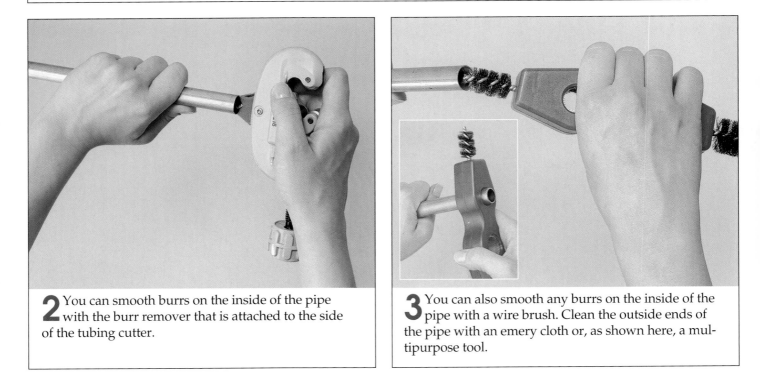

2 You can smooth burrs on the inside of the pipe with the burr remover that is attached to the side of the tubing cutter.

3 You can also smooth any burrs on the inside of the pipe with a wire brush. Clean the outside ends of the pipe with an emery cloth or, as shown here, a multipurpose tool.

Soldering Copper Pipe

Use only lead-free solder (nickel or silver) for pipes that carry drinking water. Protect your eyes with safety goggles and your hands with work gloves. Get a 12 x 12-inch piece of sheet metal to insert between the joint to be soldered and any nearby wood.

1 Brush on Flux. Use a small brush to coat the joint ends with flux. Slide the fitting over the pipe ends so that half of the fitting is on each pipe.

2 Heat the Pipe and Fitting. Heat the joint by running the torch's flame over the fitting. Don't burn the flux.

The pipe will heat up also; when it is hot enough to melt the solder, take the torch away, and feed solder into the joint until it won't take any more.

3 Protect Surfaces. If you are soldering near combustible surfaces, place a section of sheet metal between the soldering area and the combustible surface to prevent fires. You can also use a flame shield, which is a fireproof woven fabric.

4 Test the Joint for Leaks. Cool the pipe with a wet rag; then test the joint for leaks. If leaks develop, try adding more solder. If more solder doesn't stop the leaks, melt the joint apart using the torch and start over.

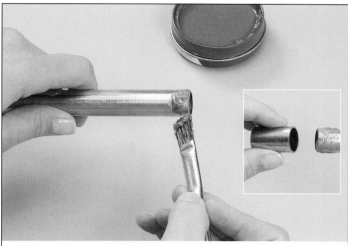

1 Coat the pipe ends with flux using a small brush. Insert the fitting over one pipe end. Twist the fitting to spread the flux. Then connect the second pipe to the fitting.

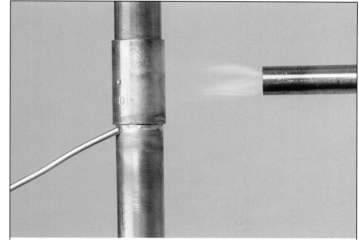

2 Light the torch, and begin to heat the fitting. Heat the fitting until it is hot enough to draw solder into the joint. Continue until the joint is filled.

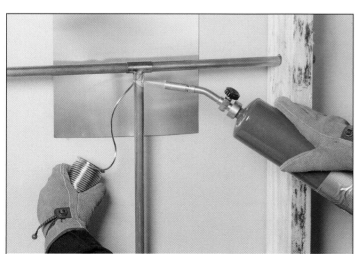

3 To prevent fire, place a small piece of sheet metal between the area you are soldering and any combustible material.

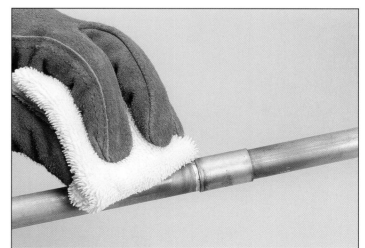

4 Wipe the pipe with a rag to clean the joint. Check your work for leaks. Stop leaks with more solder. If that doesn't work, melt the joint apart and try again.

Drainpipe Systems

In most cases, you should be able to install a new plumbing drain system using PVC (polyvinyl chloride) plastic pipe. If the existing DWV system consists of cast-iron pipe, you'll have to use a neoprene fitting to join the two. (See opposite.)

Connecting Plastic Pipe

1 Cut the Pipe. You can use any saw to cut plastic pipe, but a fine-toothed tool provides the cleanest cuts.

2 Trim the Edges. Use a utility knife to clean up the cut edges of the pipe. Even the sharpest saw will leave burrs and shavings. You can also use a medium-grit sandpaper.

3 Apply Primer. Applying plastic pipe adhesive is really a two-step process. Begin by brushing on a primer. Be sure to coat the entire area.

4 Apply Liquid Cement. Brush cement onto mating surfaces. Work in a well-ventilated area.

5 Join Pipe Sections. Join sections together, and give the fitting a quarter turn to spread the adhesive evenly. The adhesive actually melts the surface of the pipe, fusing the surfaces together as the adhesive cures.

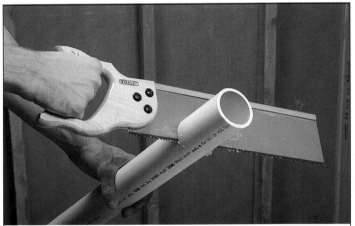

1 Cut the plastic pipe (supply lines, drains, and vents) using almost any saw. A fine-toothed blade like a backsaw's makes a cleaner cut. For cuts close to a wall you can use a flexible wire saw.

2 When you cut through plastic, even a fine-toothed saw can leave burrs and small shavings. Trim them off inside and out. A utility knife or medium-grit sandpaper works well.

3 You can use one coat of adhesive in many cases, but it's best to start by using a primer that cleans the surface for better adhesion. Use the primer and adhesive in a well-ventilated area.

4 Apply liquid cement for plastic pipe to mating surfaces. Be sure to read and follow all label cautions. Avoid contact between your hands and the cement. It can cause serious skin irritation.

5 Plastic pipe cement softens mating surfaces. They become one when the surfaces harden. You need to work quickly. Always make a one-quarter turn when you mate pipe fittings.

Using Neoprene Fittings

Banded (no-hub) couplings are easy to use. They consist of a neoprene rubber sleeve banded by stainless-steel clamps, one at each end. Some brands use a thick but pliable neoprene sleeve and two stainless-steel clamps, while others use a thin neoprene sleeve backed by a wide stainless-steel band and two clamps. Both types are available as straight couplings; reducers, which allow you to join pipes of different diameters; and connectors such as sanitary-T fittings.

Cutting Cast-Iron Pipe

When plumbers cut cast iron, they use a snap-cutter, which consists of a roller chain that has hardened steel wheels built into it, spaced an inch apart. The chain is connected to a ratchet or scissor head. As you lever the head, the chain tightens, and the cutter wheels bite into the pipe with equal pressure, snapping the pipe in two.

The next best option for cutting cast iron is to use a reciprocating saw equipped with a suitable metal-cutting blade. Be sure to set the saw to a non-orbiting position, and use a lubricant to keep the blade from overheating.

Securing Pipes

All plumbing pipes must be secured to joists, studs, or other framing members to keep them in place, prevent bowing, and keep unnecessary stress from weakening joints. Support water pipes approximately every 36 inches of run. This helps to reduce vibration in the pipes and holds them secure when water is suddenly shut off and creates a water-hammer effect. Provide support for drain-pipes at intervals of approximately 48 inches. If need be, especially for a large toilet drainpipe, nail a 1x4 brace between joists to serve as an anchor point for the pipe's clamp, hanger, or bracket.

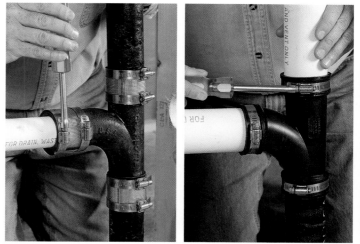

Use banded couplings (left) to splice plastic piping into a cast-iron drainage line. Install a no-hub flexible fitting (right) for greater ease in retrofitting drainpipes.

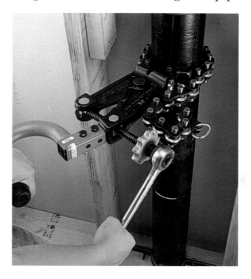

To cut cast iron, rent a chain cutter. Wrap the chain and its cutting wheels around the pipe, tighten, and twist.

Securing Pipes

Clamps and hangers are used to support pipes. Support water pipes every 36 in. or less and at every turn **(A)**. Support vertical runs of DWV pipe with riser clamps **(B)** and horizontal runs with hanger straps **(C)** at least every 48 in. Place duct tape or electrician's tape between the pipe and hanger. Horizontal overhead lengths of DWV pipe that run parallel with joists can be supported with wood braces **(D)**.

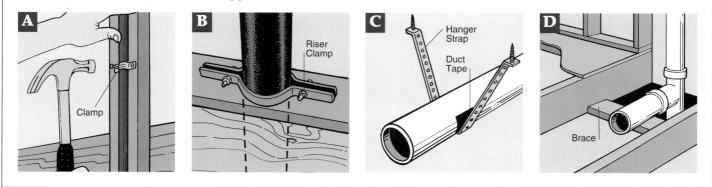

chapter 5

walls & ceilings

Finishing Walls and Ceilings

Just about any wall or ceiling surface can be used in a basement conversion, including solid-wood strip paneling, sheet paneling (plywood and others), drywall, acoustic panels, and even bare concrete block.

Painting Masonry Walls

You won't find a masonry wall, except for a large chimney, in other parts of the house, but most basements are framed with them. You can go to great lengths trying to make a basement conversion seem less like the utilitarian space it is, but maybe your goal is simply to brighten up the space without devoting too much time to the project. If maximum impact and minimum expense and effort are what you're after, consider painting the masonry walls. Poured-concrete and concrete-block walls can be successfully painted, but the paint can't cover defects. Cracks, flaws, and poor mortar joints show through just as clearly after painting as before. In fact, they may stand out even more when the walls become a consistent color. Try to make the wall as defect-free as possible by filling voids with hydraulic cement, then scraping and wire brushing the surface. If the wall is susceptible to moisture problems, the problems must be corrected first or the paint will flake off the wall. (See "Making Repairs," page 28.)

Standard latex paints are water-based, easy to clean up, and quick to dry. Oil-based products take longer to dry and require solvents for thinning paint and cleaning tools. No matter what kind of paint you use, you must clean and prime the masonry surfaces before you can begin painting.

You can paint concrete foundation basement walls with a brush, but you'll do the job faster with a roller. A short-nap roller cover, about ¼ inch thick, applies a thin, smooth layer of paint and is suitable for smooth surfaces. A longer nap, about 1 inch thick, is better for porous or irregular surfaces, such as concrete block.

Types of Drywall

Drywall, also known as wallboard, gypsum board, or by the trade name Sheetrock, is the most commonly used material because it's versatile and inexpensive. Some codes require that drywall be installed beneath other wall surfaces to provide a measure of fire safety.

Regular drywall has a gray kraft-paper backing. The front is covered with smooth off-white paper that takes paint readily, although you should coat it with a primer before applying paint. The long edges of each 4 x 8-foot sheet are tapered slightly to accept tape and joint compound. Standard drywall comes in several thicknesses: ½ inch is usually appropriate for most conversions, but ⅝-inch-thick drywall better resists bowing between ceiling joists spaced on 24-inch centers. Some kinds of drywall have special purposes. Water-resistant drywall, usually faced with blue or green paper, is made for use in areas of high moisture, such as bathrooms. Fire-resistant drywall is required by some building codes around furnace enclosures and other combustion appliances and on ceilings or walls that separate garages or workshops from living spaces.

SMART TIP

When the drywall for your project arrives, place the panels in small groups around the room. That way the panels will be where you will eventually install them. To keep them out of the way of other work, set them on edge leaning against a wall.

Drywall Types: A—¼ in., B—⅜ in., C—½ in., D—⅝ in. fire code, E—½ in. water-resistant.

Installing Drywall

You can install drywall vertically or horizontally. The goal is to install the sheets so that you end up with the least amount of joints to tape. Keep in mind that while the long edges of drywall are tapered to facilitate taping, the short edges are not tapered.

1 Make Cutouts. Electrical boxes are installed to sit flush with the face of the drywall. That requires that you create cutouts in the drywall to accommodate the boxes. Carefully measure from the edge of an adjacent sheet to both edges of the electrical box.

2 Measure Vertically. Then make vertical measurements to the top and bottom of the box. Make sure the box will sit flush with the installed sheet of drywall.

3 Lay Out the Cut. Use your T-square to transfer these measurements to the face of the drywall.

4 Cut the Opening. Then cut the opening using a drywall or keyhole saw.

5 Check the Layout. Double-check the room's framing by measuring from the corner. The edge of the drywall should fall on the center of a stud.

6 Cut the Drywall. It is easy to cut large sections of drywall. Cutting off small sections can be tricky because the edges of drywall tend to crumble. Try to plan your job so that you do not need to make small cuts. To cut drywall, transfer the dimension from the wall to the edge of the drywall. Align the T-square with the mark, and use a utility knife to score the paper facing.

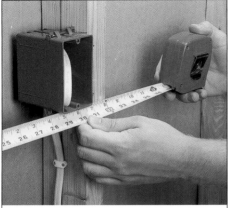

1 Measure horizontally to the edges of the box from the corner or edge of the adjacent sheet.

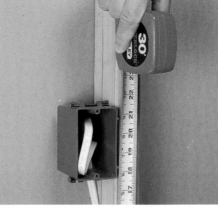

2 Measure vertically as well, noting the outside dimensions of the box, including any molded protrusions.

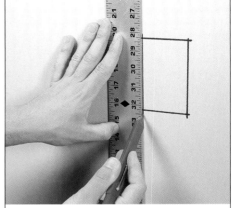

3 Duplicate your measurements on the face of the sheet, making sure you measure from the correct edge.

7 Once you score the surface, snap the sheet along the score line.

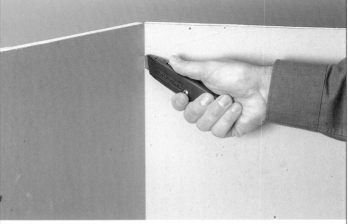

8 After you have snapped the panel, stand it on edge and cut through the paper backing using a utility knife.

7 Snap the Panel. Snap the panel along the cut. The scored side of the panel will separate cleanly. You can also snap the panel over the edge of a table.

8 Finish the Cut. Use the utility knife to cut through the paper on the unseparated side.

9 Install the Drywall. For horizontal installations, install the top panel first, butting it against the ceiling. A helper is particularly useful when installing an upper panel, but if you are working alone you can use a couple of nails to support the panel. For lower panels or full sheets on a vertical installation, a panel lifter makes the job much easier.

10 Attach the Drywall. Set the panel in place to make sure it fits properly; then set it aside, and apply a bead of adhesive to the framing. While adhesive is not mandatory, it will strengthen the installation. Set the panel back in place, and secure it with drywall screws spaced about 12 inches apart.

SMART TIP

When attaching drywall to furring strips, you will need to attach a box extender to any electrical receptacles or switch boxes that are already installed. If you don't, the boxes will not be flush with the surface of the drywall. Turn off the power; remove the faceplate; and add the extender as per the directions.

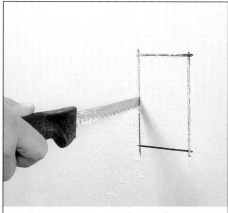

4 You can cut with a utility knife, but it's easier and safer to use a drywall saw with a plunge point to start the cut.

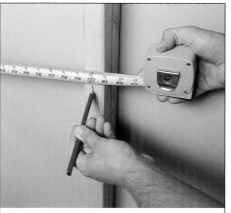

5 If your sheet doesn't reach wall to wall, measure from the corner to the center of the nearest supporting stud.

6 An oversize T-square is a handy guide for cutting. You just slice through the surface using a sharp utility knife.

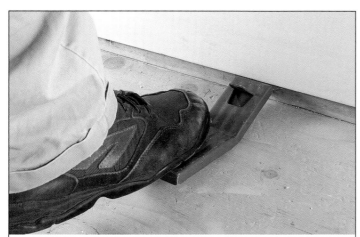

9 Use an angled panel lifter to raise the sheet against the ceiling (vertical) or upper sheet (horizontal) before fastening.

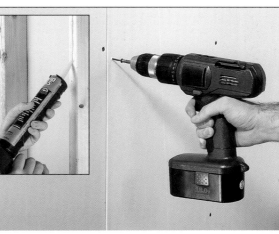

10 Apply adhesive to the framing (inset); then use a variable-speed drill to drive wide-threaded wallboard screws.

5 Walls & Ceilings

Ceiling Drywall

Drywalling a ceiling is more difficult than covering a wall because the weight of the sheet works against you. But the job is doable—even for a one-person job—if you build yourself a deadman or rent scaffolding or a panel lifter to help you manage the drywall sheets.

Using a Deadman

1 Build the Deadman. The site-built deadman is a basic T-shape that's about the same height as the ceiling. It has a foot and cap that are made of 2x4s.

2 Add a Nailer. The trick is to support one end of the sheet by installing a temporary nailer and keeping it in place while you lift the other end of the drywall panel using the deadman.

3 Lift the Panel. Place the panel in position, and apply slight pressure with the deadman. Make sure the panel remains on the nailer.

4 Install the Drywall. Drive drywall screws into ceiling joists with the deadman in place. Fasten across each joint.

Other Drywall Tools

Most do-it-yourselfers will have an easier time by renting the mechanical alternative, a panel lifter. It has a large horizontal frame to securely support a full sheet, wheels so that you can maneuver it into the perfect position, and—the best part—a big crank that smoothly lifts the sheet and presses it against the ceiling while you stroll around underneath driving nails or screws. A panel lifter won't help with the finishing process of taping and painting, but it will allow you to use the longest possible sheets.

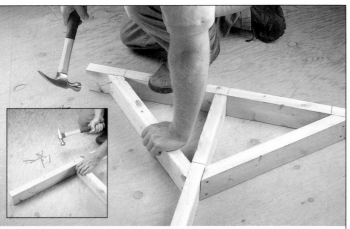

1 Build a basic T-shape support out of 2x4s. Overall height should be about the height of the ceiling.

2 Attach a temporary nailer to support one end of the sheet while you raise the other using the deadman.

3 Use the deadman for support, but keep applying pressure to prevent the panel from slipping off the nailer.

4 Drive a few nails or screws with the deadman in place. Then you can finish fastening across each joist.

Drywall Finishing

1 Check the Surface. Check for raised fasteners by sweeping a clean drywall knife over the surface of the wall. Recess any raised fasteners that you find.

2 Cover Fasteners. Apply a thin coat of joint compound to fasteners. You can cover each fastener individually, but pros prefer to cover a row of fasteners with one swipe of the knife. Give fasteners a second and third coat as you cover the joints.

3 Apply the Embedding Coat. Start filling the drywall seams by applying a coat of compound over the joint between panels.

4 Embed the Tape. Roll out a strip of tape directly over the seam. Set the tape by applying slight pressure with the knife.

5 Swipe the Tape. When tape spans the entire joint, go back and press the tape into the compound. This should leave a thin layer of compound over the tape. This important step avoids another common drywall problem—bubbles caused by dry pockets under the paper where there is not enough compound.

6 Trim the Edges. Clean up the edges of excessive compound using the knife. Try to eliminate all of the ridges in the compound.

(continued on page 82)

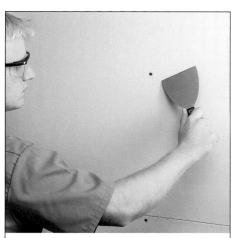

1 Start by sweeping your blade over fasteners to make sure that the heads are recessed.

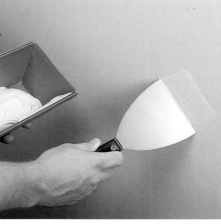

2 Use a small blade to spread compound over recessed fasteners with a back-and-forth swipe.

3 Spread and smooth out a liberal embedding coat directly over the joint between drywall panels.

4 Line up a strip of paper joint tape over the seam, and set it with light pressure from the blade.

5 Go back over the tape to be sure that it is fully embedded without any light-colored air pockets.

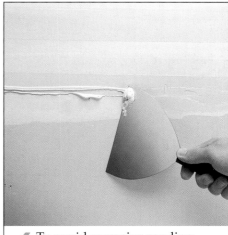

6 To avoid excessive sanding, use the edge of a blade to scrape excess material at the edges of the seams.

(continued from page 81)

7 Allow the Coat to Dry. Allow the first coat to dry. Go over the surface and sand down any high spots in the compound.

8 Apply the Second Coat. Use a 10-inch knife to apply a second coat over the first. Feather the edge into the drywall.

9 Sand if Necessary. When dry, smooth the second coat. A sanding pad attached to an extension pole makes the job easier.

10 Apply the Final Coat. The final coat should cover the first two coats. In most cases, you will need to make two passes using a wide knife.

11 Finish by Sanding. Sand all joints and fastener heads until smooth. If you have trouble producing that last smooth stroke, try wet-finishing with a sponge. Apply and smooth out the compound as best you can.

Preventing Joint Cracks

The main ways to prevent joint cracks that disrupt taped seams is to use stable studs that won't twist or warp. That means bypassing (or returning) unusually heavy studs that are overloaded with moisture. As the wood dries out, which may not happen until the first heating season, wet lumber can shrink and twist enough to pop nails and break open joints.

You also need to set framing carefully so that drywall panels will lie flat. Even small misalignments between standard studs or the extra framing installed around window and door openings can create ridges in the edges of drywall panels that rest on them. You could cover these errors with extra joint compound. But that can lead to cracking as thick coats dry unevenly.

Typical framing provides continuous support along the floor and ceiling, but not always at corners. There are drywall clips that hold unsupported drywall edges together, but in general, it's best to provide solid wood support on all drywall edges.

7 Make clean passes with a blade. You should need only light sanding between layers of compound.

8 Use a wide blade to smooth the second coat, and fill the shallow trough with feathered edges between sheets.

9 Save time sanding long seams by using a wide sanding pad on a flexible extension pole.

10 If you don't have a blade wide enough to apply a full third coat, work one edge at a time.

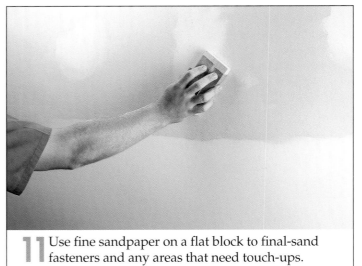

11 Use fine sandpaper on a flat block to final-sand fasteners and any areas that need touch-ups.

Standard procedure is to use paper tape where the walls form an inside corner and metal guard on corners that protrude into the room. The rationale is simple. You probably won't bang into drywall recessed behind chairs and tables but may well collide with a corner that sticks into living space. To set tape, smooth on an embedding coat, fold the tape down the center, and smooth it onto the compound using a taping knife.

Cut a length of tape to fit, and crease it down the middle.

Set and smooth the tape into an embedding coat of compound.

A metal corner guard reinforces the corner and provides a divider so that you can easily add compound on each side. You can set the guard in plumb position and nail through both flanges. On large projects, consider renting a clincher. Frequently used by contractors, this L-shaped tool automatically positions the guard and clinches small parts of the metal strip into the drywall when you hit the tool with a mallet.

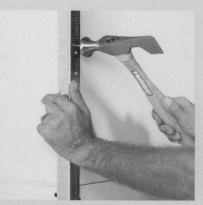

Plumb the metal corner guard before nailing it home.

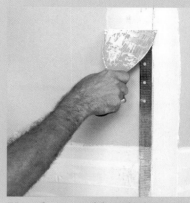

Use the metal bead of the guard to guide your knife on each side.

Painting Drywall

Cover new drywall with a primer before applying paint. Drywall manufacturers recommend a product called P.V.A. Drywall Primer, but you should ensure that the primer you apply is compatible with the paint you'll use. Purchase the same brand of primer and paint to be sure they're compatible. Primers set up wall surfaces to accept paint more readily, and paint adheres best when applied over a primer. For enamel paint, the manufacturer may recommend that an undercoat product be applied before paint.

Prime drywall before painting. If you don't, the panels will absorb paint and the paint will dry unevenly.

Acoustical Ceiling Tile

Suspended acoustical-tile ceilings have several components, including L-shaped edge strips that fasten to the walls; T-shaped main runners hung at right angles to the ceiling joists, normally from screw eyes and wires or proprietary hangers; and matching 2-foot-long crosspieces that divide the runners into a grid. A variety of different panels can fit into this framework, which covers all the seams and eliminates trimming.

1 Establish the Ceiling Height. Normally you want the ceiling as high as possible. But it may be worth a loss of ceiling height to gain room for an extra sound barrier—for example, batts of insulation. To deal with pipes or ducts dropped below the joists, pick a height that hides most of the mechanicals and requires only a minimum of extra furring or framing to box-in obstructions.

2 Planning the Layout. Because suspended ceiling grids are modular, you should make a symmetrical installation that centers the grid in the space.

3 Installing Edge Strips. Using horizontal chalk lines snapped at equal heights off the floor as a guide, nail or screw edge strips to the wall studs. At inside corners,

1 Check all the walls to find a height that will clear obstructions, and strike a level line around the room.

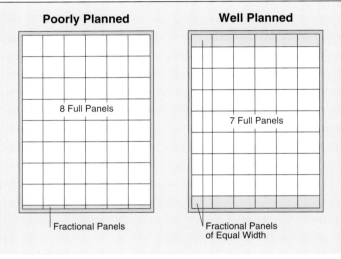

Poorly Planned

8 Full Panels

Fractional Panels

Well Planned

7 Full Panels

Fractional Panels of Equal Width

2 Adjust the layout so that border panels on opposite sides of the ceiling are the same size.

5 Runners are punched so that you can connect wire. Wrap wire around a nail on the joist, and adjust it for level.

6 Tie off the wires once the runners are level, and snap in the crosspieces that define the tile grid.

butt one edge strip against the other. On outside corners, cut the strip long and make a 45-degree miter cut to fit.

4 Installing Runners. Snap chalk lines across exposed joists to mark the location of the main runners. To test the grid for squareness, stretch strings where the runners and crosspieces will be located, and check the intersections with a carpenter's square.

5 Support the Runners. Place the main runners so that their prepunched slots for crosspieces align with your strings or chalk marks. To support the runners, insert a screw eye or nail into a joist about every 3 or 4 feet.

(Check the grid manufacturer's exact directions.) Secure using 18-gauge hanger wire inserted through the eye and through the hole in the runner directly below.

6 Add Crosspieces. Once the main runners are suspended, you simply snap the connecting crosspieces into their slots.

7 Trim the Border Tiles. Refer to your layout. Trim border tiles as needed. Cut tiles using a utility knife.

8 Install the Tiles. Now comes the easiest part of the job: installing the panels. Slide them into place on the grid.

3 Cut L-shaped edge strips to length, and fasten with screws over wall studs.

4 Lay out a grid with equal sizes of cut tiles along their edges, and install the main runners.

7 Main field tiles will tuck right into place, but you need to trim border tiles using a utility knife.

8 Slide tiles through the grid, and set them in place. You can remove them for access to pipes, wires, or ducts.

chapter 6
doors & windows

Door Styles

Along with new interior doors, your basement conversion may call for a new exterior door. This would include an exterior entrance door opening onto a stair landing if your basement is being converted into a private apartment; a new exterior basement door for both inside and outside appearance upgrades; or an additional door for convenient access to a side yard or patio. This section covers both exterior and interior doors.

As you'd see by paging through any door manufacturer's catalog, doors are offered in dozens of shapes, sizes, colors, and materials. Wood is the traditional, and still very popular, choice. Metal doors are a reasonable low-cost option for exterior doors. Exterior metal doors often feature a core of rigid foam insulation surrounded by a metal skin. The metal may be embossed or stamped to give it the look of a wood door. Fiberglass and composite doors, also produced to look like wood doors, are growing in popularity and tend to fill the price gap between metal and wood. Most wood doors are built in one of two ways: as individual panels set in a frame (called a panel door), or as a single plywood sheet, or facing, secured to each side of a wood framework (called a flush door).

Panel Doors. Panel doors offer the widest variety of choices. They can be constructed with as few as three to as many as ten or more panels in all sorts of shapes and size combinations. In some interior doors, especially those for closets, panels may be substituted with louvers, and in some entry doors, the bottom panels may be wood while the top panels are glass.

Flush Doors. Flush doors come in a more limited range of variations and are generally less expensive than panel doors because of their straightforward construction. You can enhance the simple lines of a flush door, however, by applying wood molding to its surface to give it a more traditional look. The doors consist of a surface facing, sometimes called a skin, that covers either a solid or hollow core.

French Doors. These traditional doors are framed glass panels with either true divided lights or pop-in dividers. Usually both doors open.

Sliding Doors. Patio, or sliding glass, doors consist of a large panel of glass in a wood, aluminum, or vinyl frame. The exterior of a wood frame may be clad with aluminum or vinyl. Usually, one side of the door is stationary while the other slides. Because these doors are exposed to the weather, the large expanses of glass should be double-glazed to improve the insulation value of the door.

Bulkhead Doors. These doors can provide an emergency exit, although they do not qualify as a bedroom egress under building codes. A bulkhead door also provides convenience. It's easier to get furniture into the basement if the pieces don't have to be lugged through the house. If the basement is going to be used as a shop, a door is essential for getting plywood, lumber, and large tools inside.

Adding a door for a basement is a big job: it involves cutting a large hole in the foundation and pouring concrete retaining walls to hold back the earth—a job best left to the professionals.

Bulkhead Doors. The steel panels of the bulkhead door protect the stairwell from weather. An insulated steel passage door keeps heat in the basement.

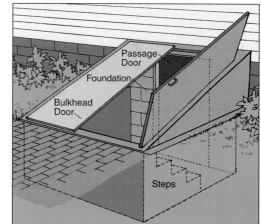

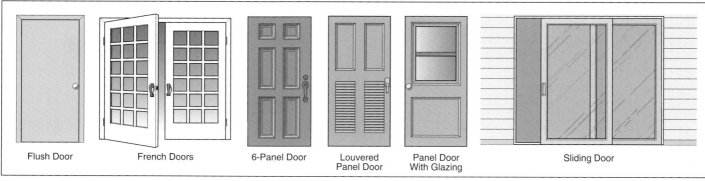

Flush Door   French Doors   6-Panel Door   Louvered Panel Door   Panel Door With Glazing   Sliding Door

Door Styles. Doors vary in appearance and construction, as well as in the way they open and close. Their designs vary to suit different functions and architectural styles.

Prehung Doors

If you want to add a door to a room, selecting a prehung door can make the installation simple and quick. With a prehung door, you eliminate the need to fit the door to the opening, to cut mortises for the hinges and lockset, and to fit the door stops. All the really fussy and time-consuming work is already done for you, and for the beginner or pro, this can be a real advantage.

Most lumberyards and home centers carry a variety of door styles for prehung applications. In addition, you can often choose between pine jambs that can be painted or stained, or hardwood jambs, with red oak being the most common choice. Interior doors can have a flush design—with a flat veneered or fiberboard surface—solid wood panels, or molded fiberboard panels. Of course, it is also possible to custom order a more unusual combination of

door and jamb and have it prehung for you.

When ordering a door, you will not only need to specify the style, material, and size, but also the direction you wish the door to open. The convention that applies to this issue is as follows: if you open the door toward you and the hinges are on the right side, the door is a right-handed door; if the hinges are on the left when it opens toward you, it is a left-handed door.

The width of a standard prehung door jamb used with typical 2x4 wall framing is 4⁹⁄₁₆ inches, which allows the door jamb to just barely protrude beyond the drywall surface. This compensates for small irregularities in wall thickness.

Installing Prehung Doors

To begin your installation, remove the door from the frame by knocking out the hinge pins. You can use a nail set or

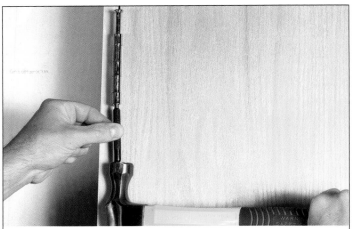

1 Use a nail set or punch to loosen the hinge pins on your prehung door. Lift the pins from the hinges, and gently pull the door free from the jamb assembly.

2 Stand the jamb assembly in the door opening with both side jambs resting on the floor. Use a 24-in. level to check that the head jamb is level in the opening.

5 If the jack stud on the hinge side of the door is not plumb, you will need to use shims.

6 Drive two finishing nails near the top; then check that the edge of the jamb is plumb.

7 Be sure to use two shims, one driven from each side, to keep the jamb square.

punch to drive the pins out. Stand the frame in the opening, and check that the head jamb is level. If one side is higher than the other, block up the low side until it is correct; then note the thickness of the blocking required. Mark the bottom of the high side jamb to remove that same amount.

Test the Frame. Place the frame in the opening again to make sure that the head is level. Next, check to see if the jack stud on the hinge side of the door is plumb. If it is, use 8d or 10d finishing nails to nail the top of the jamb to the stud; then place the level on the edge of the jamb to make sure that it is plumb in both directions. Adjust the jamb as necessary, and nail the bottom. Position the nails near the top, bottom, and center of the jamb.

Out-of-Plumb Jack Stud. If the jack stud is not plumb, use a flat bar to pry the jamb away from the stud, and slip

tapered shims behind the jamb to hold it in position. To keep the jamb straight, place shims, in pairs just snug enough to keep the jamb in position, about every 16 inches along the length of the jamb. Drive nails just below each pair of shims to keep them in place. Once the hinge jamb is nailed, rehang the door and use it as a guide in positioning the opposite jamb. Place shims between the jamb and opposite jack stud to achieve a uniform gap between the door and jamb. Again, position nails just under the shims.

Test the operation of the door to make sure that it opens and closes properly. Examine the fit of the stop against the closed door. There should be no gaps at the swinging side, and a uniform gap of $1/16$ inch or less on the hinge side, so the door does not bind. Finally, use a sharp utility knife to score the shims flush to the jamb, and snap off the protruding ends.

3 If necessary, place shims beneath one of the side jambs to level the head. Measure the height of the shim; remove that same amount on the opposite jamb.

4 Cut the bottom of the high side jamb along your layout mark. A small Japanese Ryoba saw is an excellent tool for the job.

8 Re-hang the door, and use it as a guide in adjusting the latch jamb. Place shims between the jamb and jack stud to maintain a uniform gap.

9 Use a sharp utility knife to score the shims at the point where they protrude beyond the wall surface. After scoring the shim, snap it off.

Simple door and window casings help to provide a finished look to this basement bedroom.

Door Casings

Some casing styles feature mitered corners at the joints of the side and head casing; other styles use butt joints; and there are certain treatments that layer a mitered molding over butt-jointed flat stock. All styles, however, have one element in common, and that is called a reveal. Instead of fastening the casing flush with the door side of the jamb, it is traditional to hold it back to allow a small, uniform margin of jamb to be exposed on its edge. The setback is known as the reveal, and this treatment applies to window casing and door casing alike. The actual dimension of the reveal you use is up to you, but $\frac{1}{8}$ to $\frac{5}{32}$ inch is typical. If the reveal is too large, you reduce the amount of jamb available for nailing the casing, and if it is too small, even the smallest discrepancy becomes visible. Whatever measurement you decide to use, it is important that you make it the standard for the entire job so that you maintain a uniform look throughout. Use a combination square as a gauge, and place light pencil marks at the corners, center, and ends of your jambs to indicate the amount of setback.

Evaluate the Condition of the Door

Begin by making sure that the head and side jambs are level and plumb. When you check the side jambs, use a long straightedge with the level to span the entire jamb length. Then use a framing square to check the head and side jambs. If you find that the corners are not square, use a sliding bevel gauge to determine the actual angle. Transfer the angle to a piece of scrap lumber or cardboard; then use an angle gauge to measure the angle. Use one-half of that angle for your miter saw setting to cut the corner joint.

Simple Colonial Casing

The one-piece "Colonial" casing is one of the simplest treatments for door and window casing. Along with the "clamshell" or "ranch" molding, it is one of the standard choices for homebuilders throughout the country. The techniques for either type are essentially the same. In a mitered casing installation, the desired result is a continuous and seamless border of molding around the door opening. Begin by laying out the jamb reveals at the top corners, bottom, and midpoint of the jamb. Next, cut a miter on one end of the head casing stock and hold it in place, aligning the short end of the miter with one of the reveal marks on the side casing. Use a sharp pencil to mark the short point of the opposite miter on the other end of the molding.

Attach the Head Casing. Cut the piece to length, and tack it in place by driving 4d finishing nails driven into the edge of the jamb and 6d or 8d finishing nails into the wall framing—leave the nailheads protruding at this point in case you need to remove the part for adjustment.

Cut the matching miter angles on the side casing pieces, but leave them a few inches long. Instead of measuring the side casing pieces, it is easier, and more accurate, to directly transfer the length onto the stock. Simply invert one of the pieces of side casing so that the long point of the miter rests on the floor and the outside edge of the casing rests against the long point of the head casing. Mark the length of the casing, and make the square cut. If you need to make allowance for carpet or finish flooring, simply place an appropriate spacer under the point of the casing.

Attach Side Casing. Once the casing is cut to length, spread some carpenter's glue on the mating surfaces of the miter joint, and tack the casing in place. Drive 4d finishing nails into the edge of the jamb and 6d or 8d finishing nails to fasten the casing to the framing under the wall surface. Space the pairs of nails about 16 inches apart. Check that the miters are nice and tight; then drive a 4d finishing nail through the edge of the casing to lock the joint together. Set the nailheads below the wood surface.

SMART TIP

Mark Once. As a general rule, you are always better off directly marking the size of a trim piece than measuring its length. Whenever you measure and mark a piece for length, there is an inevitable degree of variation in the way the dimension is transferred to the work piece. By marking the size of a piece directly in its ultimate location, you reduce the opportunity for careless errors.

Installing a Door Casing

1 Mark the reveal by sliding the blade on the combination square. Cut a miter on one end of the casing.

2 Align the short side of the miter with one reveal mark; transfer the opposite mark to the casing.

3 Use 4d finishing nails to tack the head casing to the head jamb of the door. Leave the nail-heads exposed.

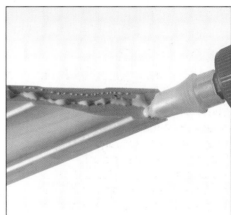

4 Cut a miter on a piece of side casing. Rest the miter on the floor or spacer (for carpet or finished floor).

5 Mark the length of the side casing pieces by running a pencil along the top edge of the head casing.

6 Apply a small bead of glue to both miter surfaces. Nail the side casing to the jamb and wall framing.

7 Drive a 4d finishing nail through the edge of the casing to lock the miter joint together.

8 Use a nail set to recess the nailheads about ⅛ in. below the wood surface.

Installing Basement Windows

When it comes to basement windows, the key is to make the most of what you have. First, repair or replace damaged windows. Then trim the windows to fit the decor of the new room.

Unless yours is a daylight basement (a basement with at least one wall exposed to the grade), it probably does not have much by way of windows. For a recreation room or a home office, this isn't a problem. Simply wire the room so that it has plenty of artificial light. For rooms used as bedrooms, however, building codes come into play.

Building Codes and Basement Windows. Building codes require that all bedrooms, including those in a basement, have a means of emergency egress.

If there's a door that leads directly outside (and not to a bulkhead door), it can be considered an emergency exit. If there's no door, however, each bedroom must have at least one egress window. The requirements for such a window specify its minimum height (24 inches), its minimum width (20 inches), its minimum "net clear opening" (5.7 square feet), and the maximum distance between the sill and floor (44 inches). The net clear opening is measured between obstructions, such as window stops, which restrict passage. Window manufacturers usually specify which windows meet egress standards.

Replacing a Wood Window

One problem with wood-framed basement windows is that they're susceptible to rot and insect damage. In some cases the affected wood can be simply cut away

and repaired with epoxy wood filler. Extensive damage calls for replacement of the entire window. Measure the size of the rough opening, and check local window sources to see whether replacement windows are readily available. If not, you will have to order a custom-built window. The new window may take some time to arrive, so don't remove the old window until the new one is in hand. Replacement methods vary depending on how the original window was installed; so pay attention as you remove the old one to how it was secured in the opening.

Window Details. With most basement windows, the frame is flush with the inside surface of the foundation wall. If the inside of the foundation is to be insulated, however, the window has to be "boxed-out" so it matches the combined thickness of insulation and finished wall surfaces. Given the variety of window sizes, frame types, and locations, there's no one best way to box a window. If the window provides egress, check with local building officials before proceeding—boxing out a window sometimes affects its accessibility.

Boxing a Window

For wood-framed walls that are built to insulate the foundation (secondary walls), there are several ways to finish the area around the foundation windows. The simplest way is to treat the window as if it were in a standard frame wall. A 2x4 sill nailed between studs forms the rough opening while the ceiling butts into the top of the window. The new jambs and sill may be finished with paneling or drywall. Remember to consider their thickness when you install the framing.

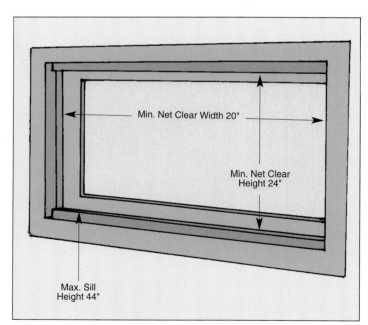

Building Codes and Basement Windows. An egress window is used as an emergency exit. The net clear opening can't be less than 5.7 sq. ft.

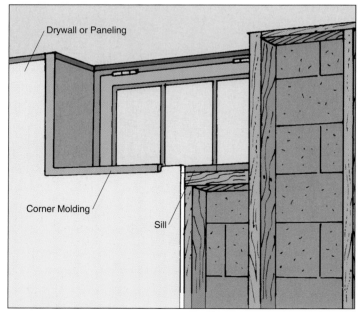

Boxing a Window. In places where a secondary wall meets a window, you can detail the framing to support finished wall surfaces.

Beveling the Windowsill

An alternative to boxing out a recess is to bevel the windowsill. Beveling the sill takes planning and some carpentry skills but results in a brighter basement because it allows sunlight to spill into the room.

1 Frame the Wall. To provide clearance for the beveled windowsill, the wall framing immediately beneath the window must be shorter than it would otherwise be. For a 45-degree bevel, the wall must be shorter by the width of the studs (3½ inches, for example, if you're framing with 2x4 lumber). For a steeper bevel, the wall must be even shorter. Frame out the wall; tip it into place; and fasten the bottom plates to the floor and the top plates to the underside of the joists.

2 Add Blocking. Cut 1x4 blocking to the width of the window, and attach it to the foundation with masonry screws. Don't use nails when you're working this close to the edge of the masonry. Cut a 45-degree bevel on a length of one-by or two-by stock that's the same length as the first piece, and nail it to the sill on the framed wall to provide support for the sill panel. You can bevel the top edge of the blocking as well, if you like.

3 Install the Sill Panel. The sill panel can be plywood, drywall, or even paneling to match surrounding paneling. In any case, cut a piece to fit beneath the window and tack it temporarily in place. You may have to take out the panel and trim it slightly after the finished wall surfaces have been installed.

After installing the finished wall surfaces (usually drywall or plywood paneling), trim the sill panel as necessary for a good fit. Put fiberglass insulation behind the panel; then nail the panel to the support and the blocking underneath. Add a small horizontal sill to cap the top of the panel. You can make the transition between the sill plate and wall by installing corner bead.

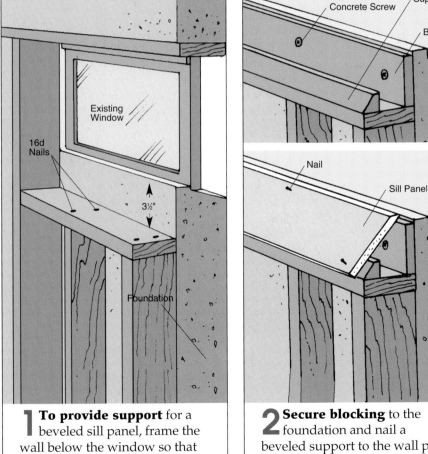

1 To provide support for a beveled sill panel, frame the wall below the window so that its top plate is lower than it would otherwise be.

2 Secure blocking to the foundation and nail a beveled support to the wall plate (top). Cut the sill panel and tack it into place (bottom).

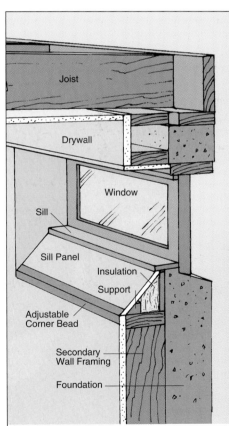

3 Cut the sill panel to finished size; add insulation behind it; and nail the panel into place. Trim the beveled area as needed.

Installing Window Wells

It's possible to fit a small window at the top of a foundation wall and still maintain the mandatory 6 inches above grade (the code minimum). The code is intended to protect wooden building elements from rot by keeping soil away from them. If the windows are too close to the soil, try to lower the nearby grade level. Make sure the ground still slopes away from the foundation. The soil you remove can probably be used elsewhere in the yard. If you can't lower the grade, you'll have to install a window well.

A window well works like a dam to hold soil away from a window that's located partially below grade. Although you can build a well with concrete block, you might find it easier to use a galvanized steel product purchased from a home center. The ribs in a galvanized steel well give it strength, and flanges at each end allow it to be bolted to the foundation walls. Wells come in various sizes. Choose one that's at least 6 inches wider than the window opening and deep enough to extend at least 8 inches below the level of the windowsill.

1 Dig the Hole. To allow room for gravel, dig 4 or 5 inches deeper than the depth of the well. The top of the well must be about 6 inches above grade.

2 Mark Bolt Locations. Hold the well against the foundation, and mark the position of the mounting holes. Coat the contact areas with asphaltic mastic, and install the well. Backfill the outer perimeter with pea gravel; then shovel 4 or 5 inches of pea gravel into the well itself to improve drainage. To keep out accumulations of snow and debris, cover the well with a clear plastic cover.

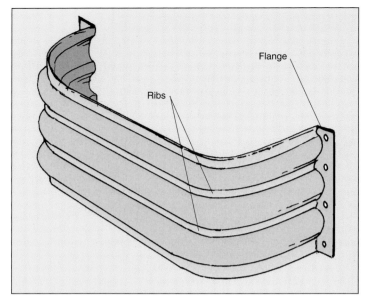

Installing Window Wells. Choose a well that's 6 in. wider than the window opening and deep enough to extend at least 8 in. below the window sill.

SMART TIP

You can leave the window well uncovered as shown here, or cover it with a clear plastic cover made for that purpose. The cover is sloped to shed rain and to keep leaves and other debris out of the well, but it will still allow light to penetrate into the basement. Be sure to buy the right size cover for your window well.

1 Dig a hole that's big enough to contain the window well. Allow several inches of leeway to maneuver the well into position.

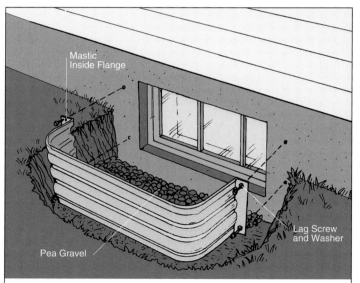

2 Use the well as a template to mark bolt locations on the foundation; then drill for masonry anchors. After the well is installed, backfill it with pea gravel.

Window Trim

Some aspects of window trim are identical to those on door trim. Casing details, once established for any particular job, are applied equally to both types of opening. However, there are some features of each that are particular. Of course, plinth blocks are only relevant in a discussion of door casing. In similar fashion, window stool, aprons, and extension jambs are particular to window trim. And there is an optional treatment with windows that does not apply to door openings—the picture-frame casing, or casing that surrounds all four sides of the opening.

Extension Jambs

To prepare a window for casing, the first step is to determine whether you will require extension jambs. Because exterior walls are framed at different thicknesses and receive different interior wall treatments, the finished depth of an exterior wall can vary considerably from job to job. Instead of offering windows with different jamb widths, most manufacturers rely on the trim carpenter to adapt the windows to the site by applying extension jambs to the window. Some window companies offer stock that has an interlocking profile, but most allow for site-built extensions using ¾-inch clear pine or hardwood.

Installing Extension Jams

1 Use a straightedge and ruler to measure the depth of required extension jambs. Check the measurements at several places around the frame, and use the largest dimension.

2 If extension jambs are wider than 1¼ in., it is best to assemble them into a frame before installing them to the window. Drill and countersink pilot holes, and screw the parts together.

3 If there is no insulation around a window, use nonexpanding foam to fill any gaps before installing the extension jambs. When the foam sets, you can easily cut off any excess.

4 Place the extension jamb assembly into the window opening, and align the inside surfaces with the factory window jambs.

5 Use trim screws to fasten the extension jamb assembly to the factory window jambs. If you center the screws in the edge of the jambs, the holes will be covered by the casing.

Establish the Extension Size. Use a small straightedge to measure the distance between the edge of the jambs and the wall surface. Sometimes a window is installed so that it is not perfectly parallel with the wall surface, so check the dimensions at several spots around the window frame and use the largest measurement. Ideally, the jambs should be about 1/16-inch proud of the wall.

Once you determine the width of the extensions, use a table saw to rip them to width. If at all possible, maintain one factory edge on each jamb to minimize edge preparation, and mount that edge facing into the room. Jambs that are less than 1 1/4 inches wide can be nailed directly to the factory jambs; just drill pilot holes through the stock to keep the nails going straight, and to avoid splitting. If the extensions need to be wider than 1 1/4 inch, it is best to assemble them into a frame and then use long trim-head screws to fasten the entire assembly to the window. If you are concerned about keeping the extensions perfectly flush to the factory jambs, you have the option of creating a small reveal between the parts.

Troubleshooting. Sometimes, the distance varies between the factory jambs and wall surface at different spots around the perimeter of the window. If the difference is small, less than 1/8-inch, pick the greatest measurement and cut all extensions to that dimension. You can take up that discrepancy with shims and caulk or by skim-coating the wall surface. If the difference in dimension is great, you can plane the strips to follow the wall surface.

Stool and Apron

The traditional approach to window trim involves the installation of a wide, horizontal shelf-like member at the bottom of the window. Many people mistakenly refer to

this piece as a window sill; however, the correct term is window stool. (Sill refers to the angled exterior portion of the window designed to shed water and snow.) Stools are generally cut from 5/4 stock. You can sometimes purchase dedicated stool stock from a millwork supplier; this material will usually have a molded profile along its front edge, and sometimes an angled rabbet that is designed to sit over the sloped window sill.

However, it is a simple matter to fabricate your own stool stock, either with or without a molded edge, from 5/4 lumber. The stool extends past the window jambs onto the wall surface—these extensions are known as horns. The horns support the side casings, and generally extend about 3/4 inch beyond the casing on both end and face. The gap between the wall surface and the bottom of the stool is covered by a trim piece called an apron.

Add Extensions. Older windows require extensions only on the top and sides as the stool could rest directly on the interior portion of the sill. On newer windows, it is often appropriate to install extension jambs on all four sides of the window—even when a stool will be used. On these windows, the sill only extends to the exterior portion of the window, so the bottom extension provides support for the stool and eliminates the need for separate blocking.

Casing Reveals. Gauge the eventual position of the outside edge of the side casing by taking a piece of casing stock and holding it on the reveal mark. Place a light mark on the wall surface to indicate the outside edge of the casing; then place another mark 3/4 inch outside that line to indicate the end of the stool. Repeat this process on the opposite side of the window. Measure the distance between those marks on either side of the window to arrive at the overall stool width; then crosscut the stock to length.

The horns of the window stool extend beyond the edges of the side casing.

Lay Out the Horns. Hold the stool blank against the wall with its ends on the outside gauge marks. Use a square and sharp pencil to mark the locations of the inside surfaces of window jambs on the stool. Then, measure the distance between the stool and the window sash. In some cases, the distance may be different at each end of the sash. In these situations, use the larger measurement and plane the leading edge of the stool to fit later.

The ends of the stool that project beyond the sides of the window and onto the wall surface are called the horns. Use a square to extend your measurement marks onto the stool surface to indicate the cuts for the horns. Calculate the overall depth of the stool by adding the casing thickness plus ¾ inch to the horn layout line.

Trim the Horn. Use the table saw to rip the stool to the desired width. Next, use a hand saw or jig saw to make the cutouts for the horns. Test the fit of the stool in the opening. On some windows, you will need to make further notches and rabbet cuts to accommodate window stop and specialized weather-stripping. The horns of the stool should sit tight to the wall surface and there should be a uniform gap between the sash and the stool of about ¹⁄₃₂ inch. You can easily gauge the gap by slipping a piece of cardboard between the sash and stool. Use a sharp block plane to adjust the fit of the stool against the sash.

Shape the Edge. Use a router to shape the desired profile along the front edge and ends of the stool. It is perfectly acceptable to use a roundover, chamfer, or ogee profile for the stool. Just select a shape that works well with the casing of the windows. If you are not comfortable cutting a profile on the relatively narrow end of the stool, you can always create a mitered return to carry the profile back to the wall surface. And if you prefer a simpler treatment, just use a sanding block to ease the sharp edges of the stool.

Install the Stool. Place the stool in the opening, and place shims under it, if necessary, to adjust its position. The stool should be level, so use a spirit level to check it. Then, fasten the stool to the sill or bottom jamb with 8d finishing nails. It is also a good idea to nail through the horns of the sill into the wall framing, but if you do so, be sure to first drill pilot holes for the nails.

Apply the desired casing to the sides and head jamb, following the methods discussed for door trim. The casing should rest firmly on the stool, but otherwise, the treatment is the same whether a window or door is involved. The stock for the apron can be the same as that used for the window casing, or you can use an entirely different profile or a combination of two or more moldings. The overall length of the apron should be the same as the distance between the outside edges of the side casings—generally 1½ inches shorter than the stool. If you use flat stock for the apron, you can simply cut it to length with square cuts at the ends. If you choose profiled stock, you should cut mitered returns on the ends to continue the profile back to the wall. Hold the apron in place, and check that it fits tightly to the bottom side of the stool. If the stool is not perfectly flat or if the apron stock is not perfectly straight, it may be necessary to plane the top edge of the apron so that there is no gap between the parts. Fasten the apron to the wall using 8d finishing nails; then drive two or three nails through the stool into the top edge of the apron to lock stool and apron together.

Windows and doors are not the only items that benefit from the application of trimwork. Here molding frames a set of built-in shelves.

Installing a Stool and Apron

1 Align a piece of casing with the reveal mark on window jambs, and mark its outside edge on the wall. Place another mark ¾ in. away to indicate the end of the window stool.

2 Hold stool stock in place against the window, and use a square and sharp pencil to mark the inside dimensions of the window jambs onto the stool surface.

6 Use a saber saw or handsaw to cut the notches at both ends of the window stool.

7 Place the stool blank in the window opening to mark any additional notches required to fit around window stops. Some windows may require a rabbet.

10 Shape the inside edge and ends of a window stool with a router and bit of your choice. It is common to use roun-dover, chamfer, or ogee profiles.

11 Use 8d finishing nails to fasten the stool to the window jamb or sill. If necessary, place shims beneath the stool to keep it level.

3 Use a combination square to gauge the depth of the notch for the horns on the window stool.

4 Hold the body of the combination square against the edge of window stool stock; then run a pencil along the end of the blade to lay out the cutout for the horns.

5 Place a piece of casing stock along the cutout line; mark along its front face. Add ¾ in. to determine the overall width of the window stool.

8 This detail of the notch and rabbet on the edge of the window stool accommodates the jamb and a stop.

9 To avoid any binding between window sash and stool, you need to provide a gap of about 1/32 in. Use cardboard to test the gap. If necessary, trim the leading edge of the stool.

12 Drill pilot holes through the edge of the horns before driving 8d or 10d finishing nails to fasten the stool to the wall framing.

13 Cut mitered returns on the ends of apron molding stock. Apply glue to both surfaces of each miter joint before assembling the parts.

14 If necessary, use a sharp block plane to trim the top edge of the apron so that it fits tight to the stool.

chapter 7

flooring

Installing Plywood Underlayment

The correct underlayment will make your new flooring stay flat and resist water for many years. First prepare the existing slab so that it provides a solid vapor-tight base. (See pages 42–43.) Then check your flooring manufacturer's instructions to select the correct underlayment thickness. Cut the panels to size, and place them on the subfloor so the joints are staggered.

1 Cut the Plywood. To cut plywood underlayment, place the panel on scrap boards; mark the length on both edges; and snap a chalk line between the two marks. Make the cut using a circular saw. Be sure to set the blade depth so the saw cuts through the panel but doesn't hit the subfloor.

2 Stagger the Joints. Start the second course with a sheet that's shorter than the first, so the joints in the underlayment are staggered. Maintain a ½-inch expansion joint between sheets and along room walls.

3 Attach the Underlayment. Panels should be attached to the structural floor supports, not just the subflooring. Lay out where the supports fall, and snap chalk lines above each. Drive screws that reach at least 1 inch into the supports.

1 Place the plywood on a sturdy base for cutting. Set the saw blade so that it cuts through the plywood but does not hit the subfloor.

2 Place the plywood so that joints between sheets are staggered. Leave a ½-in. space between sheets and along the wall.

3 Drive screws through the plywood, the subflooring, and into the subfloor supports. Select screws long enough to penetrate 1 in. into the supports.

Checking the Room

The biggest obstacles to installing floor tile are applying tile to an out-of-square room, a floor that isn't level, or a room whose walls are not straight. If you identify the problem before you begin work, you can usually fix it—using the least visible wall to absorb the trouble, for example.

1 **Check for Square.** The best way to check a room for square is to use a 3-4-5 right triangle. Measure from the corner along one wall to the 3-foot point and mark the floor. Do the same with the other wall, but mark the floor at 4 feet. If the diagonal distance between these two marks is 5 feet, the room is square.

2 **Check for Level.** Level is another room characteristic you should check. Do this by placing a 4-foot level on a long 2x4. If the floor is more than ½ inch out of level in 10 feet, it will be noticeable where the wall meets the floor. Because of this, it's a good idea to avoid using tile on the floor and the walls.

3 **Check for Straightness.** Do this by running a string between same-sized blocks nailed to both ends of the wall. Then run a third block, of the same thickness, between the string and the wall, and mark where the wall isn't parallel with the string.

1 Measure out 3 ft. along one wall and 4 ft. along an adjacent wall. If the distance between the two points is 5 ft., the corner is square.

2 Check a floor for level by placing a 4-ft. level on top of a straight 2x4. If the floor is ½ in. out of level, don't use tiles on the floors and the walls.

3 To determine if a wall is straight, tack blocks connected by a string on each end of the wall and move a block between the two.

Flooring Layout

Before planning a layout for new flooring, make sure that the floor is reasonably square (opposite.) If the walls are less than ¼ inch out of square in 10 feet, it will probably not be noticeable. If they are more than ¼ inch out of square, the condition will be visible along at least one wall, and you'll need to make angled cuts. Try to plan the layout so that the angled tiles are positioned along the least noticeable wall.

Making Working Lines

If you're installing any kind of tile flooring, plan the layout so that a narrow row of cut tiles does not end up in a visually conspicuous place, such as at a doorway. Often, the best plan is to adjust the centerline so that cut tiles at opposite sides of the room will be the same size. If you start by laying a full row of tiles along one wall or if you start laying tiles from the centerline, you can end up with a narrow row of partial tiles along one or both walls. To correct this, shift the original centerline, or working line, a sufficient distance to give you wider cut tiles at both walls.

Layout for a Square Room.
If the room is relatively square, snap a chalk line along the length of the area down the center of the room. Then snap a second chalk line across the width of the room so that each chalk line crosses in the center of the room. Check the cross with a framing square to make sure that the intersection forms a 90-degree angle. You can start tiling at the intersection and work toward the walls.

Creating a Diagonal Layout.
When laying tiles diagonally, a second set of working lines is required. You'll need a chalk line at exactly 45 degrees from your vertical and horizontal working lines, but don't be tempted to just snap a line from the center point to the corner. Your layout won't work because your new working lines won't be exactly 45 degrees from the vertical and horizontal lines.

You will need a measuring tape and a pencil to lay out the diagonal lines. From the center point, measure out an equal distance along any two of the lines, and drive a nail at these points, marked A and B on the drawing below. Hook the end of a measuring tape to each of the nails, and hold a pencil against the measuring tape at a distance equal to that between the nails and center point. Use the tape and pencil as a compass to scribe two arcs on the floor that will intersect at point C. Snap a chalk line between the center point and point C; then do the same thing on the other side of the room.

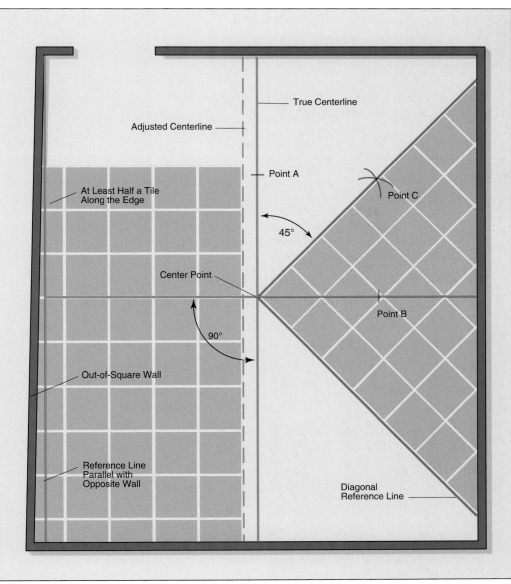

Carefully snapping chalk layout lines before you begin to install the flooring will help you to make a balanced, symmetrical layout. The blue lines indicate the lines for a standard layout; the red lines for a diagonal layout.

Installing Vinyl Floor Tiles

1 **Prepare the Layout.** Set tiles working from the middle of the floor outward. (See "Making Working Lines," page 103.) Use a framing square to make sure the intersection of lines is square. Adjust chalk lines as needed.

2 **Setting the Tiles.** Spread adhesive with a notched trowel held at about a 45-degree angle. Drop tiles in place. Use a rolling pin to apply pressure to the tiles in each row as you set them.

3 **Trim Edge Tiles.** When you come to a wall and can no longer set full tiles, place a dry tile on top of the last set tile from the wall. Then put a third tile over these two tiles, pushed to the wall. Scribe the second tile using the edge of the topmost tile as a guide.

4 **Trim around Corners.** Repeat step 3. Without turning the tiles, keeping them in the same position, slide them to the right of the corner and align them on the last set tile. Mark it the same way. Cut the marked tile to remove the corner section.

1 Lay the tiles out on the work lines. If the fit isn't right, adjust the lines. Place a row of tiles along each of the chalk lines to check your layout.

2 Spread adhesive; apply it with a notched trowel held at a 45-deg. angle (top). Drop the tiles into place. Use a rolling pin to embed the tiles (bottom).

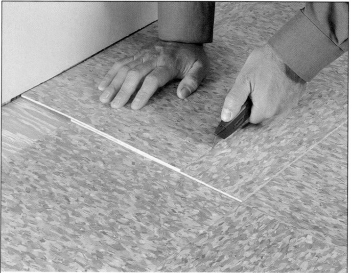

3 To cut a border tile, place a tile over the last full tile, and place another tile on top of it, butted against the wall. Cut where the top two meet.

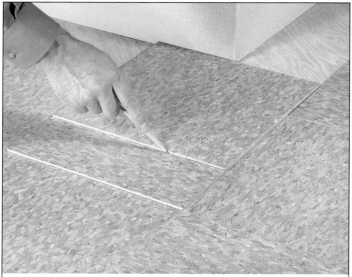

4 To cut around a corner, repeat step 3; then move to the other side of the corner, and realign the pieces to make the second cut.

Installing Ceramic Tile

1 Draw Layout Lines. You can apply tile to the slab or to a subfloor. Snap chalk lines to establish working lines. Spread adhesive using a notched trowel. Apply only that which you can cover before the adhesive sets.

2 Install the Tiles. Place the tiles in position, and maintain spacing between tiles. Use a straightedge to make sure that tiles are aligned. Seat tiles by tapping them lightly with a carpeted-covered wood block.

3 Apply Grout. After adhesive has cured, apply grout using a rubber float. Work diagonally across the field of tiles to work the grout into all seams. Follow the manufacturer's directions regarding the grout's set time, and don't allow the grout to cure for too long.

4 Clean Grout Haze. Grout residue will form a light haze on the face of the times. Remove it by cleaning with a damp sponge. Rinse and wring-out the sponge frequently until the haze is gone.

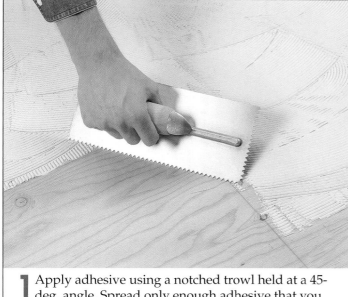

1 Apply adhesive using a notched trowl held at a 45-deg. angle. Spread only enough adhesive that you can cover with tile before the adhesive dries.

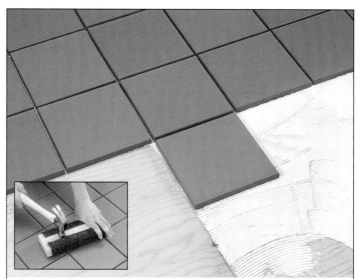

2 Give tiles a slight twist as you set them in the adhesive. Seat tiles by tapping them lightly with a carpeted-covered wood block (inset).

3 Apply grout using a rubber float held at a 45-deg. angle. Sweep the grout into seams by working diagonally across the face of the tile.

4 Remove grout haze by rinsing with clean water. Follow the manufacturer's directions on when to start rinsing. Soak and wring out the sponge frequently.

Installing Laminate Flooring

1 Install First Rows. Cover the insulated subfloor (pages 42–43) with the foam padding. Align the first few rows of flooring, using spacers to maintain the gap along the wall.

2 Glue Planks. Follow the manufacturer's instructions carefully. Apply a continuous bead of the approved glue along either the groove or the tongue of the plank. Push the planks together, and tap them into position.

3 Use Clamps. After laying at least three complete rows, use strap clamps to hold them firmly together. Don't skip the clamping when using a glue-down system. Snap-together laminate flooring does not need to be clamped.

4 Install Last Rows. Trim the final row of planks as you would any type of strip flooring or tile. Place a plank over the last completed row; insert another plank or scrap plank against the wall spacers. Use this line to scribe a cut line. Glue as described.

1 Roll out the foam; then test-fit the first three rows, stepping the planks. Apply a bead of glue to the length of the tongue or groove on the edges and ends.

2 Use a tapping block to drive the planks into position. Look for excess glue that beads up along the seam of the plank, and remove it with a plastic putty knife.

3 Use strap clamps to hold just-glued planks together. Lay at least three complete rows, and allow the glue to set up for about one hour before continuing.

4 To cut final planks, lay a plank over the last installed one. Use a third plank or a piece of scrap to scribe a cutting line on the good piece.

Installing Sheet Vinyl Flooring

1 Lay Out and Cut the Flooring. It is best to lay this flooring over an insulated subfloor (pages 42–43). Unroll the flooring in a room big enough to lay out the whole sheet. With a marker, draw the room's edges on the flooring; add an extra 3 inches on all sides. Cut the flooring to the marks using a straightedge and a utility knife. Position the piece so about 3 inches of excess goes up every wall.

2 Trim Flooring. Crease the flooring into the joint at the wall with a 2x4. Then place a framing square in the crease, and cut with a utility knife, leaving a gap of ⅛ inch between the wall and the flooring. To trim outside corners, cut a slit straight down through the margin to the floor. Trim inside corners by cutting the margin away with increasingly lower diagonal cuts on each side of the corner.

3 Adhere and Seam. Roll back the flooring to the center, and apply adhesive to the exposed half of floor with the smooth edge of a notched trowel, following the manufacturer's directions. Roll out the flooring immediately onto the adhesive. Repeat for the other half of the flooring. If a second or third sheet of flooring must join the first, stop the adhesive about 2 inches short of the edge to be seamed when installing the first sheet. Spread adhesive on the floor to receive the second piece, stopping about 2 inches from the first sheet. Position and align the second piece carefully, allowing it to overlap the first piece slightly. With a sharp utility knife, cut through both sheets along the seam line. Remove the waste. Peel back both edges, and apply adhesive. Press the flooring into place. Use the seam sealer recommended for your flooring. Press the flooring firmly into the adhesive with a roller.

Vinyl flooring is available in a variety of colors, textures, and patterns.

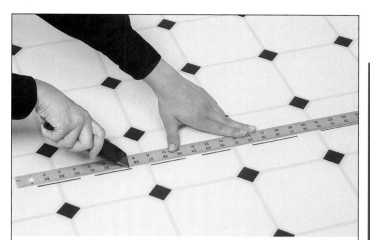

1 Make the rough cut with a knife and straightedge in an area where you can lay out the entire piece of flooring.

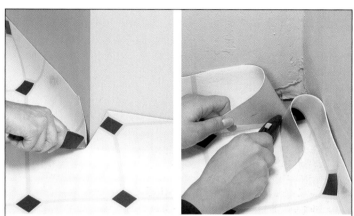

2 To trim outside corners, slit the margin down to the floor with a utility knife (left). On inside corners, cut diagonally through the margin until the flooring lies flat (right).

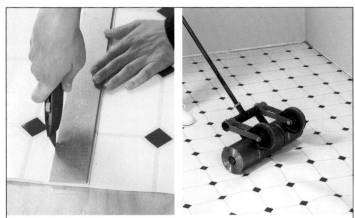

3 To make a seam, apply adhesive up to 2 in. from the edge of the first piece. Overlap the two pieces by 2 in. Cut through both pieces, and remove the waste (left). Seal with a seam roller (right).

Installing Base Molding

You can install base trim before or after installing the finished floor. If you trim before installing the floor, use spacers as shown. The techniques vary for inside corners, below, and outside corners, opposite.

1 Make a straight cut. Inside corners require a coped joint so that the profile of one piece of trim fits over the profile of the adjoining piece, creating a tight joint. Start by butting one piece of baseboard into the corner.

2 Make a coped cut. Coped cuts take some practice. First use a miter saw to cut an open 45-degree bevel—an open bevel has its long point on the back surface of the stock, exposing the profile of the molded surface. Then use a coping saw to cut along the exposed profile. (See "Cutting Coped Joints," below.)

3 Attach the molding. When the joint fits snugly, use finishing nails to attach the baseboard to each wall stud and the wall plate near each stud. Never attach base trim to flooring. Set nails using a nail set.

Cutting Coped Joints

Set the coping saw blade so that it cuts on the pull stroke. Many people like to outline the profile in pencil so that it stands out. Keep the blade about 1/16 inch to the waste side of the profile. Manipulate the saw so that it follows the profile of the molding. Once you make the cuts with the saw, use a rasp or file to refine the cut.

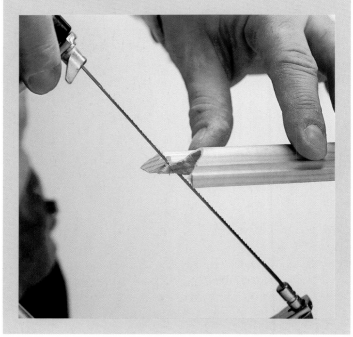

1 Make a straight cut on one piece of baseboard, and butt it into the corner.

2 Using a coping saw, cut a coped joint the adjoining piece of baseboard.

3 Attach the molding by driving nails into the wall studs and the wall plate. Do not nail molding to the flooring.

Installing an Outside Corner Joint

Because drywall is not a precision material, outside corners may not be perfectly square. Before you cut the molding stock, it is good idea to test fit scrap lumber at the corners. That way you can make adjustments without wasting stock.

1 Test the angle. Cut a 45-degree bevel on the ends of two pieces of 1x6 stock. Hold them together around the corner. If the joint is not tight, make the necessary adjustments. If the joint is open at the outside, increase the angle of the cut slightly. If the joint is open at the wall, reduce the angle of the cut. Both pieces of the miter joint should have an identical angle.

2 Cut the baseboard. Place masking tape on the floor around the corner; mark the outside face of the baseboard. Hold stock for each side of the joint in place. These lines mark the long point of each miter.

3 Test fit the baseboard. Do a dry run before attaching the baseboard. When satisfied, nail one side of the corner using finishing nails or a pneumatic nailer. Drive a nail at each stud.

4 Attach the second piece. Apply glue to the surfaces of the miter joint. Attach the second piece to the wall. Use 4d finishing nails or brads to pin the joint together.

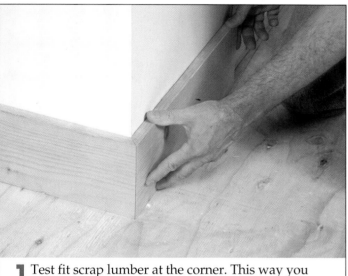

1 Test fit scrap lumber at the corner. This way you can make adjustments before cutting the baseboard.

2 Mark the outside face of the baseboard on painter's or masking tape attached to the floor.

3 When the joint fits tightly, attach one side of the corner to the wall.

4 Apply glue to the joint; attach the second side to the wall; and pin the joint using finishing nails or brads.

glossary

Actual dimension The exact measurements of a piece of lumber after it has been cut, surfaced, and dried. Example: A 2x4's actual dimensions are 1½ x 3½ inches.

Building codes Municipal rules regulating safe building practices and procedures. Generally, the codes encompass structural, electrical, plumbing, and mechanical remodeling and new construction. Confirmation of conformity to local codes by inspection may be required.

Butt joint A joint in which a square-cut piece of wood is attached to the end or face of a second piece.

Cable staples Heavy-duty staples driven into framing and used to support cable when running wire.

Circuit breaker A protective device that controls an electric circuit, cutting off the power automatically when a given overcurrent occurs. Can also be operated and reset manually.

Conduit Metal or plastic tubing designed to enclose electrical wires.

Drywall Also known as wallboard, gypsum board, or plasterboard; a paper-covered sandwich of gypsum plaster used for wall and ceiling surfacing.

DWV (drain, waste, vent system) The system of piping and fittings inside the walls used to carry away plumbing drainage and waste.

Ground-fault circuit interrupter (GFCI) A safety circuit breaker that compares the amount of current entering a receptacle on the hot wire with the amount leaving on the white wire. If there is a discrepancy of 0.005 volt, the GFCI breaks the circuit in a fraction of a second. The device is required by code in areas subject to dampness such as bathrooms, kitchens, and outdoor areas.

Header A structural member that forms the top of a window, door, skylight, or other opening to provide framing support and transfer weight loads. Header thickness should equal wall width.

Inspection Whenever a permit is required, it is necessary to schedule a time for a city or county building inspector to visit your home and examine the work.

Jamb The inside face of a window or door liner.

Joist One in a series of parallel framing members that supports a floor or ceiling load. Joists are supported by beams, girders, or bearing walls.

Load-bearing wall A wall that is used to support the house structure and transfer weight to the foundation.

Miter A joint in which the ends of two pieces of wood are cut at equal angles (typically 45 degrees) to form a corner.

Nominal dimension The identifying dimensions of a piece of lumber (e.g., 2x4), which are larger than the actual dimensions (1½ x 3½).

On center A point of reference for measuring. For example, "16 inches on center" means 16 inches from the center of one framing member to the center of the next.

Partition wall A wall that divides space. It may be load-bearing or nonload-bearing.

Penny (abbreviated "d") Unit of nail measurement. Example: A 10d nail is 3 inches long.

Permit A license granted by a local building department that authorizes extensive construction work on your home. Minor repairs and remodeling work usually do not call for a permit, but if the job consists of extending the water supply and the drain, waste, vent system, adding an electrical circuit, or making structural changes to a building, a permit may be necessary.

Polyethylene sheet A plastic material well suited to retard vapor passage in a floor, wall, or ceiling. Common thicknesses are 4, 6, and 8 mils.

Post A vertical support member. In a basement, the post typically provides intermediate support for a beam or girder. In most cases, the concrete slab immediately beneath the post has been thickened to form a footing that distributes the structural loads.

R-value A number assigned to thermal insulation to measure the insulation's resistance to heat flow. The higher the number, the better the insulation.

Radon A colorless, odorless radioactive gas that comes from the natural breakdown of radioactive metals in soil, rock, and water. When inhaled, molecules of radon lodge in the lungs and may lead to an increased risk of lung cancer.

Rigid insulation Boards of insulation that are composed of various types of plastics. Rigid insulation offers the highest R-value per inch.

Service entrance panel The point at which electricity provided by a local utility enters a house wiring system.

Sistering The process of reinforcing a framing member by attaching another piece of lumber alongside it.

Sleepers Boards laid over a concrete floor as a nailing base for the subflooring of a new floor.

Soil pipe The main drain line of a house, it conducts water and waste away from the house. Typically, it is the largest pipe in the basement and may be plastic or cast iron.

Stud Vertical member of a frame wall, placed at both ends and most often every 16 inches on center. Provides structural framing and facilitates covering with drywall or plywood.

Subfloor The floor surface below a finished floor. Usually made of sheet material such as plywood; in older houses, it is likely to consist of diagonally attached boards.

Sump pump A device that draws unwanted water from a sump pit and pumps it away from the house.

Toenail Joining two boards together by nailing at an angle through the end, or toe, of one board and into the face of another.

Top plate Horizontal framing member, usually a 2x4, that sits on the top of wall studs and supports floor joists and rafters.

Underwriters Laboratories (UL) Independent organization that tests electrical products for safe operation and conformance with published standards under various conditions. Products that pass may display the UL logo.

Vapor barrier Material—usually plastic—used to block the flow of moisture vapor.

Window well Made of concrete blocks or galvanized steel, a hollowed area that holds soil away from a window that is located partially below grade.

index

Glossary/Index

Photo Credits

Illustrations by: Clarke Barre, Craig Franklin, Robert LaPointe, Ed Lipinski, James Randolph, Frank Rohrbach, Paul M. Schumm, Ray Skibinsky, Ian Warpole

All photography by John Parsekian/CH, unless noted otherwise.

page 1: Henry Wilson/Redcover.com, design: Voon Yee Wong **page 3:** *top* Olson Photographic, LLC; *center* Tony Giammarino/Giammarino & Dworkin; *bottom* Olson Photographic, LLC, design: Greyrock Companies **page 5:** *top left* Tony Giammarino/Giammarino & Dworkin, design: 2north.net; *top right* Olson Photographic, LLC; *bottom* Anne Gummerson **page 6:** *top left* Todd Caverly, design: Lorraine Construction; *top right* Todd Caverly, design: Rockport Post & Beam; *bottom both* Olson Photographic, LLC, design: EHL Kitchens **page 7:** Jessie Walker **page 9:** Olson Photographic, LLC, design: Kitchen and Bath Design, Stonington, CT **page 10:** Olson Photographic, LLC **page 11:** *top* Jessie Walker; *bottom* Olson Photographic, LLC **pages 13–14:** *all* Brian C. Nieves/CH **page 16:** Todd Caverly, design: George Snead Jr. **page 18:** *top left* Todd Caverly, design: G.M. Wild Construction Inc.; *top center* & *bottom* Olson Photographic, LLC; *top right* Tony Giammarino/ Giammarino & Dworkin, design: 2north.net **page 26:** Phillip H. Ennis, design: Beverly Ellsley **page 30:** *bottom* Olson Photographic, LLC **page 31:** *all* Merle Henkenius **page 33:** Jessie Walker **page 35:** *all* Merle Henkenius/CH **page 37:** *top* Elizabeth Whiting Associates; *bottom* Anne Gummerson, design: Rhea Arnot Design **page 38:** *top left* Eric Roth, architect: David Pill Architects; *top right* Olson Photographic, LLC, design: Kling Bros Builders; *bottom* Olson

Photographic, LLC **page 45:** courtesy of Timber Frames by R.A. Krouse **page 49:** Olson Photographic, LLC, design: Brindisi & Yaroscak **page 50:** *all* Freeze Frame Studio/CH **page 52:** Olson Photographic, LLC, design: Complete Construction **page 53:** Neal Barrett/CH **page 56:** *all* Olson Photographic, LLC; *top left* & *bottom left* design: Amazing Spaces; *top right* design: Kitchen and Bath Design, Stonington, CT; *bottom right* design: Heminway Construction **pages 57–60:** *all* Brian C. Nieves/CH **pages 61–62:** *all* Freeze Frame Studio/CH **pages 63–64:** *all* Brian C. Nieves/CH **page 65:** *all* Merle Henkenius **pages 67–69:** *all* Brian C. Nieves/CH **pages 72–73:** *all* Freeze Frame Studio/CH **page 75:** *top both* Merle Henkenuis/CH **page 76:** *all* Olson Photographic, LLC; *top right* design: Kling Bros Builders **page 78:** *bottom right* Freeze Frame Studio/CH **page 83:** *top bottom* Freeze Frame Studio/CH **page 86:** *top both* Olson Photographic, LLC; *bottom* Tony Giammarino/Giammarino & Dworkin, design: 2north.net **pages 88–89:** *all* Neal Barrett/CH **page 90:** Olson Photographic, LLC, design: Nancy Budd Interiors **page 91:** *all* Neal Barrett/CH **page 95:** *all* Neal Barrett/CH **page 96:** *left* Neal Barrett/CH; *right* Olson Photographic, LLC, design: Sally Scott Interiors **page 97:** Olson Photographic, LLC, design: J Interiors **pages 98–99:** *all* Neal Barrett/CH **page 100:** *all* Olson Photographic, LLC, *left* design: RMS Construction, *top right* design: Kling Bros Builders, *right center* design: Country Club Homes **page 101:** *all* Freeze Frame Studio/CH **page 102:** *all* John Parsekian/CH **pages 104–106:** *all* Freeze Frame Studios/CH **page 107:** *bottom left* courtesy of Armstrong; *right all* Freeze Frame Studios/CH **page 108:** *left all* Neal Barrett/CH; *bottom right* Gary David Gold/CH **page 109:** *all* Neal Barrett/CH

Metric Conversion

Length

1 inch	25.4 mm
1 foot	0.3048 m
1 yard	0.9144 m
1 mile	1.61 km

Area

1 square inch	645 mm²
1 square foot	0.0929 m²
1 square yard	0.8361 m²
1 acre	4046.86 m²
1 square mile	2.59 km²

Volume

1 cubic inch	16.3870 cm³
1 cubic foot	0.03 m³
1 cubic yard	0.77 m³

Common Lumber Equivalents

Sizes: Metric cross sections are so close to their U.S. sizes, as noted below, that for most purposes they may be considered equivalents.

Dimensional lumber	1 x 2	19 x 38 mm
	1 x 4	19 x 89 mm
	2 x 2	38 x 38 mm
	2 x 4	38 x 89 mm
	2 x 6	38 x 140 mm
	2 x 8	38 x 184 mm
	2 x 10	38 x 235 mm
	2 x 12	38 x 286 mm
Sheet sizes	4 x 8 ft.	1200 x 2400 mm
	4 x 10 ft.	1200 x 3000 mm
Sheet thicknesses	¼ in.	6 mm
	⅜ in.	9 mm
	½ in.	12 mm
	¾ in.	19 mm
Stud/joist spacing	16 in. o.c.	400 mm o.c.
	24 in. o.c.	600 mm o.c.

Capacity

1 fluid ounce	29.57 mL
1 pint	473.18 mL
1 quart	1.14 L
1 gallon	3.79 L

Weight

1 ounce	28.35g
1 pound	0.45kg

Temperature

Celsius = Fahrenheit – 32 x ⅝
Fahrenheit = Celsius x 1.8 + 32